adanu

Helping That Helps
Empowering Ghanaian Communities

By Richard Yinkah

with Shelly Morse and Karen Lynn Maher

Adanu: Helping That Helps—Empowering Ghanaian Communities
By Richard Yinkah with Shelly Morse and Karen Lynn Maher

Adanu.org

ISBN: 978-0-9992884-2-9 (Print Book)
ISBN: 978-0-9992884-3-6 (Ebook)

Library of Congress Control Number: 2017954788

Cover design by O'Daniel Designs
Batik design on the cover by the Amenuveve Batik Center, Woadze Tsatoe, Ghana
Interior text design and printing by Gorham Printing
Printed in the United States of America

Kirkland, WA
legacyoneauthors.com

In Ewe, the language spoken by the people of the Volta Region of Ghana, adanu means "wise collaboration."

"when you climb a good tree"
Adinkra symbol of support, cooperation, and encouragement

CONTENTS

" Yes, we build schools, but schools are just the beginning. Through these schools we build hope, because education is the critical bridge to a lifetime of genuine opportunity in Ghana. "

—RICHARD YINKAH

FOREWORD

I was first introduced to Adanu when I traveled with a small team of faculty and staff from Michigan State University (MSU) to the Volta Region of Ghana in the summer of 2017. We were making a site visit to local communities where Adanu has been supporting partnerships among village residents and international university students to establish elementary schools, libraries, and other projects. During our site visit Adanu's founder Richard Yinkah described the Adanu model. Far too often, he explained, rural people in Africa are told—and come to believe—that they have nothing to contribute to their own development. Adanu's approach is different; they engage with local communities directly as partners who have valuable resources and ideas.

Yinkah asks them, "Don't you have sand, rocks, and water for the bricks? Don't you have trees for timber? Don't you have labor to offer?" Indeed, on the day we visited a school site in Adaklu-Hehekpoe near Ho, men and women of all ages were carrying building materials and preparing the foundation for a new classroom they were building.

At the same school, we passed a classroom where two young American women from Alma College (Alma, Michigan) were teaching a kindergarten class. The children were learning a song about rain as part of an English lesson. The classroom was sturdily built with plastered brick walls and an iron roof, and it was freshly painted. There was a garden and playground equipment. The Alma College students told us that they were initially on a study program and decided to return on their own to continue their work as volunteers. One of the young women was interested in education, while the other wanted to learn about "how to help." She wanted to understand the principles and best practices that guide meaningful community-based engagement for change.

Adanu's approach to building schools and supporting meaningful partnership among Ghana's rural communities and American university programs resonates deeply with Michigan State University's legacy and future vision. It also corresponds with the values that guide our commitment to community engaged learning. The participatory approach that Adanu uses—working with communities to identify their challenges and assuring all partners join together in developing solutions—has strong synergies with our MSU values. Community engaged learning at MSU seeks to prepare our students for lifelong civic and social responsibility in an increasingly diverse and complex global society. Our approach is to address the challenges that face global communities through collaboration with those communities. We also encourage the critical, reflective thinking that is required to enhance academic skills and generate impactful, sustainable outcomes. We don't think of *service* and *critical thinking* as separate activities. All truly beneficial service must incorporate thoughtful reflection; likewise, critical thinking has the greatest impact when it is done in a context of global social connection.

Michigan State University looks forward to our ongoing collaboration with Adanu through global community engaged programs for learning, research, and ethical practice. During our visit to Ho we experienced synergies that will connect our Study Abroad, African Studies, and faculty research teams, including our higher education partners such as the University of Ghana. Adanu is the bridge to creating meaningful partnerships with rural communities, community organizations, and academic institutions committed to making a difference.

Education at all levels is taking place in the Volta Region in the classrooms where American students like those from Alma College are teaching. This education has global impact because of the relationships created in Ghana. University students travel back to Michigan and share what they have learned with others. Together we are cooperating to lay the foundations for the classrooms of the future, both in Michigan and in Ghana.

—**Jamie Monson**, Director of African Studies and
Professor of History, Michigan State University

PREFACE

When Richard Yinkah started a small organization in his aunt's home, he had a dream of creating better opportunity for communities in Ghana. Step by step, he pursued his vision to build schools as a way to bring opportunity to the Volta Region, Ghana. From its humble beginnings, Adanu has now grown into a sizeable organization with multiple volunteers, staff, sponsors, partners, and stakeholders.

As you read this book, I invite you to learn from Richard's example. From nothing, he created a sustainable model that is positively changing the culture of Ghana. His quest proves that no matter how overwhelming the obstacles may be toward realizing your dreams, with vision and belief anything is possible. You can make a difference, no matter what your circumstances.

This book is a celebration of Adanu's collaborative success over the past fifteen years. Though written in Richard's voice to enable the reader to follow Adanu's story more easily, it is an effort of many hands and voices. Shelly Morse's partnership and experience is especially reflected throughout its pages. (Her personal reflection is shared in the Afterword.) Comparable to Adanu's model of collaborative community, every team member and person in the book has played an integral part in bringing this story to life.

A passionate tale about never giving up, holding fast to a vision, and triumphing over incredible odds, this book reveals the courage, conviction, and patience it takes to develop meaningful change and purpose in the world. I've been deeply inspired by Richard's story. His discovery of combining practical Western best-practices with the heart and soul of Ghana has truly created a model that brings opportunity to his homeland and firmly establishes a path to sustainable change. There is no better legacy.

As any entrepreneur knows, all projects start with an idea, but the work often brings different results than the original plan. Crafting this book has been this type of journey for me. Its scope and promise of far-reaching impact has been a pinnacle in my career, both personally and professionally.

When I visited Ghana on behalf of this book, I was surprised how joyfully I was greeted by the local people. Blanketed by this effusive love and kindness, I asked, "Why are they so happy I'm here?" I was told it was because I was there to give them a voice so they could become visible to the outside world. They told me their happiness stemmed from knowing someone cared about them and that others in the world would know they exist because of this book. Their appreciation moved me deeply.

I was struck yet again with the human need to share our stories. The people and the communities I met in Ghana want to be known. The importance of the written word as a conduit for communication, connection, understanding, and change has never been more apparent to me. Crafting this book has been a training ground for listening beyond simply hearing their words, most of which were spoken in Ewe.

There is deep caring, intercultural exchange, and love wrapped into the Adanu's work with communities. Volunteers, donors, partners, and other stakeholders not only sustain the organization, they also build lasting relationships with the communities they serve. Everyone works together for the good of the common goal. No project sustains itself on money alone. The community spirit exemplified by Adanu is both profoundly moving and effective.

Motivated by a higher calling to create opportunities for marginalized communities, Adanu's model of collaborative community participation inspires possibility, hope and confidence. Because of help from Adanu and its partners Ghanaian communities build and sustain their own opportunity.

I am honored and delighted to share what this organization gives to the world. Beyond the pure exhilaration involved in telling the story, it has also inspired my philanthropic commitment. The experience has been life-changing. I hope it is for you too.

—**Karen Lynn Maher**

Answering a Call to Serve

Success comes from believing you can make it. You can do it! So don't give up.

—Richard Yinkah

Mother Africa. Birthplace of civilization. Place of my heartbeat. Place of my heartache. Rife with lack of opportunity and political strife, Africa has more than its share of problems. Lack of access to quality education is rampant. Villages are isolated and lack school buildings or trained teachers. Even if schools are within driving distance, transportation is unreliable or completely unavailable. Village sanitation and the proper environment for learning is severely lacking. Learning is a struggle.

But the joy of the heart rises there anyway. Ghana is rich in love, kindness and generosity. Strong in joy. We are one body, one community. The rhythm we share together is a dance of one people and one heart. When I give to you, I am blessed. When you give to me, you are blessed. When we share with each other, the community is blessed. We are enlightened in one body, one mind, one soul, one world. Our children's happiness is our joy. When you are with us, your presence is also our joy. This deep, human connection is central to how we live. We freely share it with open arms.

Ghana is where the sweet smell of dry grass and tundra shrub wafts through the pleasant, cool high mountain air. It's where my heart opens amidst the low, pulsing dance of women in brightly-colored waist wrap skirts, their feet rooting into the earth. Ghana is my home. I am called daily to respond to the lack of opportunity here and provide more access to education for my people. I'm inspired to bring them more visibility in the world and a better life.

With this spirit and intention, in 2002 I founded an organization called Disaster Volunteers of Ghana (DIVOG), now known as Adanu. Westerners call it a philanthropic organization. To me, it's my life's calling. We build schools throughout the Volta Region because education opens doors of opportunity for Ghanaians and changes lives for the better *forever*. Education connects us to the outside world and equips the leaders of tomorrow to address current problems and needs. Education is the foundation for hope. When people are educated they become aware of their capacity for self-sufficiency and independence; they realize they have the resources to solve their own problems and build better economic systems from within. They develop confidence.

Collaboration is the guiding principle of Adanu. Hand in hand, with help from outside, Adanu helps Ghanaian communities drive their own change. Every individual and community has something valuable to contribute to improve their lives.

This book is a story that celebrates Adanu's 15-year anniversary. It's meant to enlighten readers about how education leads to sustainable opportunities for individuals and communities. In these pages I share Adanu's model of collaboration, which is designed to create a future for the Ghanaian people that is filled with hope. Helping communities build an educational infrastructure is how Adanu provides *helping that helps* to end an historic lack of opportunity felt throughout the beautiful country of Ghana.

Many Ghanaian communities feel they have no voice or personal power. A culture of fear and mistrust and a tendency to remain invisible within the borders of their own communities is a common experience. Focused daily on survival, not thriving, they look outside of themselves for immediate solutions. But real change comes from within. Teaching communities to rely on themselves changes this dependency on others and gives villages a sustainable model of community involvement to support long-term solutions. Lasting change comes from believing that they already have the necessary resources for change.

At Adanu, we hold fast to the ideal that personal participation leads to sustainable problem solving and development skills, and ignites thriving communities. Education is the key to that growth. To that end, we foster empowerment and collaboration, not charity, within the villages we serve. This kind of partnership and consensus building takes time to build. We know that sustainable and long-lasting change requires repeatable systems, accountability, and tangible measurement of what works and doesn't. Our approach facilitates the openness, willingness, and ability of communities to adapt to a collaborative model of community development.

Most of all, at Adanu we feel change requires a full, open, and recognized heart. People need to know that what they think and feel matters, that they can contribute to decision-making that affects their lives, and that they are stakeholders in creating their communities. The experience of having their say—being asked their opinion, speaking honestly, and being heard—brings them out of isolation and empowers them to take charge of their lives.

People ask me why I do what I do. The short answer is: I choose to do God's work. It's a blessing. I believe I was put here by God, and my destiny and Adanu's mission is to serve others. Every member of our team brings individual gifts to Adanu, and each of us is a gift to each other. We could not do this without each other. From day one, I've never given up and I never will.

My family and many of my friends don't understand why I am doing this work because I could make more money doing something else. But I've chosen this. I don't want my kids to go through the same struggles I endured. I want them to have a better life. Education is the key. Ghana's children will navigate their own paths, but I'm going to do my best to give them the educational tools they need to have a better life. Adanu is the vehicle I've chosen to travel the path laid out in front of me.

Within this book is the heartfelt story of why I founded Adanu, what it does, and my vision for the future. It includes my perspective and shares first-hand accounts with Ghanaian individuals and communities about how their relationship with Adanu has been transformative.

There's an African proverb that says, "Hold a true friend with both hands." Here, I extend both of my hands to you and invite you to share in the joy of Adanu.

—**Richard Yinkah**

PART I

Adanu's Origin

"help me and let me help you"
Adinkra symbol of cooperation
and interdependence

CHAPTER ONE

The Adanu Model

Since its inception, Adanu's goal has been to improve the standard of living for the rural poor in Ghana. We build schools to improve the education infrastructure, the foundation of opportunity, personal empowerment, and hope.

First through trial and error, and now through careful studies of what works, we bring development and improvement to their lives. Adanu's model of collaboration brings noticeable improvement quickly. This model gives rural people the opportunity to play an active role in their communities' growth and transformation. From start to finish, communities are directly involved in leading and working on all projects.

Adanu's impact is so much more profound than just the building of a school and a community infrastructure. Our model works because we make long-term commitments to the communities we serve so that what we build is sustainable. Community members do the work, agreeing that improving children's access to education is their common goal. We teach people that they have their own resources of time, energy, and skill to get the work done. We help them make wise choices for the overall good of the community. The resulting self-respect and personal dignity is the secret sauce to our work.

We rely on individual volunteers and donors, corporations with a philanthropic mission, and academic institutions with service-based international study programs to help us bring about lasting change throughout the rural communities of Ghana's Volta Region. We can't do our work in isolation; we hold these committed partnerships in high regard. When a community has a proper school, our government feels compelled to provide trained teachers, effective learning materials, desks and chairs, electricity, and more. Our partners provide funding that makes this possible.

I have worked to develop The Adanu Model with my team for over fifteen years. The main areas are: *Community Selection, Community Engagement*, and *Community Partnerships*. We focus on projects in rural communities that need improved infrastructure, particularly in education.

Community Selection

The Adanu model begins with the selection of potential communities to work with. Prospective communities are identified through searches by Adanu or requests from chiefs, elders, or local and federal government officials, such as Members of Parliament or the Ministry of Education. For the past several years we have received hundreds of these requests from across the Volta Region, many of which meet our criteria, and most of which we don't currently have the funding to address.

Communities are selected based on need and their ability, willingness, and enthusiasm to give of their time, labor, skills, and basic materials. We often look at what they have already done or tried as evidence of their enthusiasm. Adanu meets with village communities to explain our model and what will be expected of them, volunteers, and other partners throughout the project.

Needs Assessment

Once we have selected a community, we guide them through a intense assessment process to determine their needs, including identifying numbers of teachers and prospective students, the condition of the existing school's infrastructure (if any), and the current availability of basic educational resources like desks, lights, toilets, and other resources such as computers and science labs. This step helps us decide whether we can meet the community's needs and if it is an appropriate project for Adanu.

Included in our assessment is determining resources the community itself can contribute. Contributions may include land, sand, water, and skilled or unskilled labor. Although they may have numerous natural resources in addition to the community's time and energy, the tricky part is convincing people that investing their own time to achieve long-term goals is beneficial. This is hard in communities where day-to-day survival is their primary focus, especially when they hear about western-based organizations and Ghanaian government agencies who have promised help that doesn't require the same type of commitment we require.

But helping community members change their mindset to focus on long-term goals is critically important. Life in these communities is driven by day-to-day survival. During the rainy season if people aren't working in the fields and spending every minute planting and taking care of their gardens, they may not have enough to eat for two months. So they are naturally reluctant to participate in building a school. Their hesitation is clearly understandable, but this type of thinking continues the cycle of poverty.

Our goal is to find communities that are willing to discover new ways to meet their day-to-day needs and achieve long-term goals for improving their community. We look for communities that are willing to give their time to a collaborative effort to improve education for their children which will have a lasting payoff. At Adanu, we emphasize that we must have a community that participates in the development of education by giving their own time, energy, and other resources. We believe this is required to create a sense of full ownership for the commitment it will take to make sustainable changes.

When a community wants to build a school, people might ask, "What do we need?" Most focus on the money. But we know there are a host of other resources needed for lasting success. That's why it's so important for us to emphasize the mindset that we are partners with the community and share in every aspect of building a school. We encourage communities to think broadly about the resources they have access to and can contribute. In rural Ghana, every community has access to sand, sun, crushed rocks, and water, all of which are necessary construction materials.

We also assess whether there are people willing to give their time, such as women who can go to the river to get water and men who can provide the necessary labor to transform the sand and water into bricks. And skilled laborers for electric, plumbing, and carpentry. But this all takes time. We start by coming into a community and identifying people who have resources and are ready and willing to work together toward a common goal. Without a community that is willing to contribute time and other resources, we cannot make the positive changes that deliver sustainable results.

Community Engagement

After we have selected and assessed a community, we move on to community engagement. We use this stage to establish expectations, ensure these expectations are clearly communicated, create leadership teams and working committees, and gather resources for the project. It is necessary to meet with all the members of a community to solicit their views and ensure buy-in on a project before we continue.

The goal is to create a team environment. For example, we don't come into a village and say, "Adanu is coming to build a classroom for you," and start pouring the cement and sand. Rather, we work with all the stakeholders of the project—the chiefs, elders, teachers, students and workers—to generate ideas and find people who can commit resources. Our goal is for members of the community to do their own problem solving. This process can take three months to a year to complete. This timeframe can be hard for the western mindset but it's crucial to the project's success.

We might ask, "If we want to make bricks with sand and water, how do we get these materials?" We don't step in with an authoritative answer, but give room for community leaders to develop and suggest their own ideas.

After a few moments, one of the community members might say, "We have them." Or someone might offer an alternate solution for reaching out to someone else for support. Adanu always emphasizes the need to have a team effort from the larger community. We want every individual to know that the end goal is achievable and that their ideas matter.

We have seen instances where the opposite mindset has completely stymied a community. Rather than working with available resources, outside groups have come in with their own money, materials, and skilled and unskilled labor. Local people aren't encouraged to band together or become invested in the project. Instead of collaborating, these villages will say something like, "Why don't you buy the sand?" or, "Why don't you pay us?" This mindset isn't empowering for people. We strive from the beginning to identify and work in a way that ensures we are creating an environment that is human-centered.

Our goal is to use resources and leadership that emanate from within the community rather than imposed by outside groups.

Once the working committees for the projects are created, the committee members decide how long the laborers will work on each project, when each project starts, how to keep the team members accountable for the resources they committed to the project, how to reward the community members, how to inform the community of the project's progress, and how to address problems as they arise. It's up to the leadership team to create the project plan.

While Adanu helps to facilitate these conversations, it is our goal to allow the members of the community to take on as much leadership as possible. The result is strong community investment in the project and the knowledge and experience to recreate these steps again in the future.

When we bring in this kind of structure to a community, the people have a full understanding of how the Adanu Model works and are empowered to move forward to address future needs, even after we are no longer involved on a regular basis. The community can lead and direct the entire process by themselves because they have been part of it since the beginning. Not only do they know how to form a group, but they also have the mindset needed to choose leaders and become accountable to each other.

For many individuals, being called to be a leader shows that the

trusts them. Leadership is a position of honor. When a com-
make that choice among themselves, everyone is accountable
r and can move forward to execute each phase of the project.

Community Partnership

The final phase of the Adanu Model is Community Partnership. This is the
working phase of a project. Adanu supervises and provides oversight at all
critical stages, checking with committee leaders regularly to keep track of
inventory, address any needs that might occur, and keep the community
accountable. Adanu may also connect international and local volunteers to
develop relationships, provide encouragement, and provide support relative
to the needs of the projects and strengths of the volunteers. Committees
chosen by members of the community determine how long volunteers will
work and the extent to which they will interact with the people.

We also work with the chiefs to help them communicate their ongoing
support for the projects to their people. When leaders and the community
don't understand why they should be contributing time and labor to build
a school, we educate them about the long-term value of community participation. This need to educate communities and their leaders about our
model is a common occurrence, but it's worth the effort. Because Adanu's
local staff are well-known and our volunteers engage at different stages of
the project, we develop committed working relationships with the people
we serve. These lasting relationships pave the way for long-term interaction
and follow-up. We are committed to staying engaged and supporting the
communities we serve.

Compared to other non-government organization (NGO) models and
programs, the Adanu Model moves slowly. But, for lasting change, our
pace is essential. This is not a typical process for projects at other NGOs.
For example, an NGO from New York connected with us and said they
wanted to start an office in Ghana. They'd read about the Adanu model and
liked it, so they came to us and said, "We like your model, but we want it
to be faster." They truly wanted to work with us. They even wanted us to
change our name to theirs, claiming if we did so we could have access to
a lot more funding and even faster results. What they didn't realize is that

focusing attention on funding sources and quick results is not aligned with our model. We cannot move faster because, if we do, we'll compromise what needs to take place to bring about lasting change.

What also makes Adanu unique and different is that we are respectful of the value and dignity of each person in the community.

We've seen how people and their villages are often unintentionally overlooked by organizations with other models that have a timeframe and schedule to keep at the expense of their relationship with community members.

In a lot of ways Adanu wants to be invisible. The project's process, timeline, and outcome are about the community, not us. We want those we serve to know that these projects are dependent on their ideas, their time, their commitment. We want them to know we will be there with support, resources, and outreach, but ultimately the result is up to them. Again, we want to send a message of empowerment.

Adanu's human-centered concept makes our community development projects sustainable. After selecting communities, we engage each one by involving them in all the various stages of the projects. We help communities see that they already have most of what they need in leadership, labor force, sand, and water to begin building a school.

This engagement affects the entire community, enabling all members to feel recognized and valued because their contribution is irreplaceable. This process makes them understand the importance of the project and motivates them to give their best effort to the cause.

The Adanu model also keeps costs down. Because the communities contribute such a large portion of the raw materials and labor through these "in-kind contributions" Adanu schools cost less than 50% of what the Ghanaian government spends when building a similar school. We also create a sense of commitment to individual projects, and empower communities to recreate this model to initiate more improvement projects on their own. We have seen this sustainability in action in many communities that have successfully completed new projects without our help, using the skills and framework of the Adanu model.

Our desire in working with communities is to get past the history of hopelessness that has been perpetuated by groups who want to help. Our communities have grown weary and weaker with organizations that try to insert a model it thinks is appropriate, but doesn't work long-term. While intentions are pure, those models often only produce short-term results.

The Adanu model helps us reach forward into the future and empower people for generations to come. This kind of cooperative change isn't just for Ghana. We aim to spread this collaborative spirit, power, and inspiration to neighboring countries, universities, and other NGOs and create lasting change, one project at a time.

Yes, we build schools, but schools are just the beginning. Through them, we build hope, because in Ghana an education is the critical bridge to a life of genuine opportunity. We also bring a style of volunteerism that makes a difference. Our volunteer trips are unique immersive experiences providing opportunities to live and work side-by-side with people from rural Ghana. Volunteers have the opportunity to become "friends-on-the-ground" with Ghanaians. The people feel that sincerity and enjoy the collaboration. Knowing someone else cares about their community and is willing to work side-by-side with them brings hope and encouragement to their lives.

By working alongside volunteers, people show increased confidence and educational improvement. They also develop meaningful friendships when conversing with others outside their community. Increased participation in the labor needed to get projects done has also been seen. People realize how educating their children will build not just a better future for their kids but also strengthen their entire community.

Communities in Ghana are recognizing the value of opening their homes and hearts to volunteers from around the world to foster understanding between cultures and provide them with access to the world outside their villages.

The Vision Behind Our Model

Far from Ghana's large capital city of Accra, the small villages of the Volta Region are connected by dirt trails and rough access roads built for the military during WWI. While the region has intermittent electricity, infrastructure is largely absent. Most villages are agrarian based communities, reliant on farming to meet their day-to-day needs. There is little to no access to clean water, electricity, healthcare, or other basic necessities. Because education is not available or is conducted literally under a tree, many parents give up and resign themselves to the fact that their children won't receive a formal education; they teach the kids to farm and take care of the daily tasks of living in the community. Thus, the projects Adanu has facilitated during the past 15 years have had a profound impact in the area. The result has been improved education, better teachers, more children attending school, improved hygiene and nutrition, and changed minds about the value of education as a way to improve the lives of community members for generations to come.

We ignite passion, opportunity, and hope in these communities. We focus on building and improving classrooms, libraries, computer labs, science labs, playgrounds, and basic level teaching learning materials (TLMs). We focus first on building schools to house kindergarten and grades 1 through 6 (students aged four to eleven). Starting early builds a strong foundation for later education success.

Our passion and motivation to focus on this age group is because almost all rural communities lack resources for the children to excel. All children are tasked with taking the same national exam as those in towns and cities that are well resourced. This makes it very difficult for rural students to pass their national exam, depriving them of their God-given potential to become responsible adults and contribute to the development of their community.

The high dropout rates in rural schools is due, in part, to rural-urban migration because parents who can afford to do so prefer to send their children to school in larger cities. This deepens the impact of poverty in rural communities. When fewer children are being educated, resources for education are diminished. However, we believe that by creating an environment within our rural communities where infrastructure, learning materials, and good teachers are provided in the schools, parents will prefer to seek education within their own communities. Additionally, quality education will empower parents and students socially. Family and community bonds will be strengthened.

The seeds of the Adanu model were already sown when we built our first school. It was our goal to use collaboration as a basis to bring about locally driven, sustainable development of communities that would usher in widespread change. Our model began to emerge when I noticed what happened all too often when well-intentioned people came from elsewhere to help communities in Ghana.

For example, a group might come to a small, rural community and build a water well, making the people there excited and happy. But then, two weeks later, something would break on the well or it would go dry. No one there knew how to fix it. If I were to go to this village and ask, "Who built the well for you?" They would respond, "Oh, some people came from the U.S. to build it for us."

"Were you involved?" I might ask.

"No."

"Do you know their company?"

"No."

Community members weren't involved in building the well nor did they have any commitment to its maintenance, so they didn't feel responsible when something went awry with a well, school, or hospital that had been built on their behalf. The same is true all over Ghana when it comes to these types of projects. As a result, communities have become distrustful of people coming in and saying, "We can help you."

When there is an endless cycle of outsiders coming in to create something and leaving without empowering local people, the communities begin to see themselves as people who are unable to change on their own.

I began to recognize that the problem lay not in the actual help, which was desperately needed, but in the way the work was being done. Organizations with good intentions were creating short-term results because their model of helping wasn't sustainable. Often these groups unintentionally hurt communities instead of helping them.

Another challenge with outside groups is they have little investment in these projects because they have limited interaction with community members. This also breeds hopelessness in our communities.

We have a saying in Ghana: "If I can do it at home, I can take it to the next-door neighbor and say, 'we can do it together'." Essentially, the saying means "charity begins at home." This is the can-do spirit that engages the community and makes them more willing to spend time, energy, and resources on a project.

In the past, usually driven by a need for funding, we've been tempted to change how we work. But we've learned we cannot compromise our model and still accomplish the full value of what we've set out to do. Saying no to faster approaches not aligned with our model has been a challenge at times. Some organizations have wanted us to adopt their model and abandon ours. We have had to say no to their partnership and funding.

We have seen our model work in the communities we serve; the results are sustainable. Daily, we see and hear the impact Adanu has on the communities we serve. We hear from the chiefs, women/mothers, students, teachers, headmasters, and government agencies touched by the positive changes resulting from their partnership with Adanu. And we are now seeing students from our schools graduate from high school and university and start to give back to their communities in meaningful ways.

By bolstering their school infrastructure, education has improved. By providing sanitation facilities and urinals, their environment is less polluted. By building fresh water supply systems, they see less illness. Moreover, by implementing the Adanu model, collaboration between the people in the communities we serve has improved. Their spirits are elevated and they are working more congenially with each other. Every community mentioned the powerful difference Adanu has made by providing them with a pathway to opportunity. All of this illustrates why Adanu's model is vitally important.

CHAPTER TWO

A Café Full of Dreams

I have always carried a positive attitude. I knew there was going to be a better day, no matter what happened, and a way out of any tough situation. This didn't mean my childhood was easy. My dad took me away from my mother when I was only five years old. He sent me to live with my grandmother near the village of Kpetoe where I started my primary school education at a Roman Catholic school. But when I was ten years old, my father died and his funeral was the only time I would see my mother again, over 27 years ago.

I relied on my faith to keep going and hope that everything would work out for the better. This is the same advice I give to young people today: to trust God, believe in themselves and don't be tempted into shortcuts. When I was growing up, I had a few close friends. One of them took a shortcut in crime, ended up in prison, and is now dead. Instead of taking the easy route, I chose the harder, more diligent path.

So, at ten-years-of-age, I moved to Ho township to live with my auntie. Growing up with her, I was keenly aware I had a different home life than my friends because she was raising me instead of my parents. She was very strict with her discipline and had no problem lighting me up with a broom when I stepped out of line.

My friends would always say, "Richard, you've got to run away!" But while there were times that sounded like a good idea, I remember asking myself, "Where would I run away to?" I didn't want to be struggling in the streets. I'd seen the tragedy of what could happen all around me. So, instead of focusing on what I couldn't handle, I decided to use school as my hope for a better situation.

In Ho, I attended primary and secondary schools. These were public schools built and run by the government. They faced similar challenges to the schools we are working to replace in villages in Ghana, such as lack of qualified teachers, dilapidated buildings, and inadequate learning and instructional materials.

The condition of the first school I attended was inferior to other public and private schools in the township. Neighborhood kids would ridicule me and call our school building a chicken coop because it had no walls. They could look straight through the classrooms and took great delight in making fun of me for attending there.

I never considered I might have better options until the results of my junior secondary school tests came in and I'd done well. For the first time, I considered the possibility that I might be able to experience a boarding school like the ones more privileged kids I knew attended. But my auntie said no because she couldn't afford the fees, a common problem in Ghana and why Adanu now builds schools in rural villages. I ended up attending another school that was no better. It carried the stigma of being a school for people from a poor home or who were unable to make good grades. Once again, other kids laughed at me.

The school I attended charged lower tuition fees, but there were still fees. Sometimes when we didn't have the money, I'd spend my days hanging out and observing people at the courthouse or post office. I kept my mind occupied by paying attention to what was going on around me in these places. It was also stimulating to assist others by helping them in some way. For example, I might give directions to someone looking for a specific room in the courthouse.

Throughout my childhood, every choice I made was for my education, even though it was a challenging journey. I didn't know it at the time, but my belief that education could help bring a future filled with hope was a gift—not just for me, but for all those Adanu has served and will serve.

Pursuing an education meant I would have to defer the financial returns available to me if I had decided to stay in the village and become a Kente weaver. But I said no to the simple way. What I've learned by going through this challenge is to never give up on yourself. There will be a way out. My biggest dream as a child was to go to school. So I kept attending classes regardless of whether I had food, shoes, or the weather was bad. I knew school was the one opportunity I could count on. Through persevering I learned that you don't have to be wealthy or have it all together to achieve a dream. Success comes from believing you can make it. You can do it! So don't give up.

My senior year, I attended St. Prospers College (a high school), another school less endowed than others in Ho. I knew if I was to make a difference in my life, I needed to be my best self. It wasn't enough to just be a member of the debate club. I wanted our debate team to win. Working very hard, I garnered winning awards for us. Even though I excelled in high school and was very engaged on campus (the drummer troop, debate club, The Red Cross), I knew my auntie didn't have the money to send me to university. Rather than seeing this as an obstacle, I was determined to better myself in everything I did, one day at a time. Throughout this entire time, I was determined to finish with good grades to open the possibility of being able to attend a university or polytechnic institution.

I survived that time in my life because I used my faith to help me stay true to who I was and who I wanted to be, rather than complaining about my situation. I could see hope ahead by focusing on my dreams and building knowledge by attending school. That foundation of hope led me forward. Once I carried the light of knowledge inside, I knew it was something no one could ever take away from me. I would carry that enlightened heart to foster change. Looking back, I realize those childhood challenges all had to happen because they taught me to be resilient and move on with purpose regardless of roadblocks that stood in my way. They taught me compassion for others going through similar struggles.

After I graduated high school, I set out to find a job where I could make money and learn as much as I could about the world. I had no idea the answer to my life's purpose would come from working in a start-up cyber café in Ho, the *Nexus International.* I went to work in the cyber café to raise money to be able to continue my schooling. It was the early 2000s, and at 19 years old, I was more determined than ever to get a university education.

Internet connectivity was brand new to Ghana. Pre-dating cell phones by many years, cyber cafés were a new, exciting way to access the world. It was a BIG deal for us to be connected to the world in this way at that time. It was a thrilling time as people came in every day, asking, "What is this whole internet thing about?" Even though I was only making seven dollars a month and oftentimes knew only just a little more than those walking through the door, working at the café became the foundation for my life's work—I just didn't know it at the time.

I never knew who was going to come in and need my services. It was intriguing to me that I was the one who was helping important doctors, lawyers, teachers, nurses, and church leaders learn how to use the Internet. I was particularly excited to be helping my fellow Ghanaian people learn about the world. I'd walk them through the process of setting up an email account, creating a password, and understanding the technology behind email. Though this is second-nature to many around the world today, at that time in Ghana, it was groundbreaking. I'd set people up with a user name and use the same password every time. To this day, there are probably 300 people walking around Ho with the same password because of me.

Working at the cyber café was a fertile learning ground as I took every opportunity to learn as much as I could from the Internet. Mypa Winfred Kofi Buckner, my supervisor, gave me an hour online every day. I read voraciously. He allowed me to print two pages of information from the web during each shift, and every day I would shrink the text to a 5-point font size to fit as much information as I could on to one page. This is probably why, even now, I am so good at reading fine print!

The more I worked at the cyber café and helped people who passed through our door, I began to notice many of them were looking for the same information. Researching non-profits, grants, foundations, volunteerism, and non-government organizations (NGOs), looking for summer camp programs. But why? Curious, I began to read alongside these people to see what they were doing.

I became interested in learning more about non-profit work. Plus, I volunteered on a Peace Corps project which was funded by local registered organizations. As I watched people research, I stumbled onto a way to fulfill my long-held desire to help the people of Ghana.

At first, I thought, "What are these summer programs? We don't have summer in Ghana." However, my interest was piqued. Before leaving the café at the end of the day, I would research more about the summer programs and why they were of so much interest to people. At that point, I started putting the pieces together for myself.

Through the programs, things were being done for communities that didn't involve reliance on government funding. And results appeared to be happening more quickly than they had through traditional means. Slowed by bureaucratic rules and lack of enough funding to fulfill the needs of communities, village leaders were turning to philanthropic organizations to fund community improvement projects, such as building schools or digging water wells.

I soon learned these summer camps were bringing in volunteers to Ghana from all over the world. People were creating school buildings, doing construction, and voluntarily helping with other labor-intensive work. I saw a disconnect between what these well-intended volunteers were doing and the benefits to the communities. The people in the communities weren't involved in the projects. I thought, "There's a lot of digging and building going on, but where are the people who will benefit from these projects?" This missing link concerned me from the beginning.

In an interest to see how these programs were truly being run, I began signing up for them. What I saw was a repeat of the same model again and again. Volunteers would drop into a community for ten to twenty days, find a classroom to sleep in, get the village excited about their work, finish the project, and then leave without any of the local people having participated in any meaningful way. The village's contribution, participation, or engagement was virtually non-existent.

After work each evening, I would go home and talk with my friend, the late Devine Agbowoada, about what I'd learned about these programs and what I'd observed. Sadly, Devine would later die after a short illness. When he and I lived in the same house, I started telling him more about my frustration with seeing all these summer programs leaving the local communities out of their projects. Over and over again, I voiced my concern.

One evening, Devine said, "It sounds as though we need to start something of our own. Why can't we start by doing something different?" Even though I felt it was something I could do, I couldn't help but wonder if I had the capacity to start an organization. And where would I get the money? With these doubts still in my mind I decided to give it a shot. Devine, Mypa (our financial manager), Robert Tornu (my childhood friend) and I founded Adanu days later.

I was certain there was a better way to help rural villages in Ghana. Based on my belief that I could do it and knowing that it was a real need, I simply said yes.

Three others also joined the team: Emmanuel Awlime, Transport Officer, a taxi driver who would prove invaluable in transporting volunteers; Ankah Angelbert Elorm (DJ), Construction Director; and Bright Kwasi Tay, Logistic Officer, my barber who took on the responsibility of operations management. He still cuts my hair to this day. None of us would receive a salary for years to come, but from the beginning we were all committed to the work.

We used the storage space inside my auntie's house for an office. She had a few random chairs and a rickety dining table with three legs. Whoever sat nearest the spot with the missing leg would have to act as the fourth leg, supporting the table on his knee while we did our work, although we had to be extra careful whenever we had guests or were hosting volunteers since the chairs were also broken. Central to our philosophy was to always give our volunteers or guests the best hospitality they deserved. It still is.

After much brainstorming, the name we came up with for our organization was the Disaster Volunteers of Ghana, or DIVOG. We were highly frustrated at seeing all the challenges in Ghana and looking at the kids who had no access to good water or quality education. Seeing these huge problems and thinking about how we would solve all of them seemed like a disaster. So the Disaster Volunteers of Ghana felt like the right name for tackling the issues we were trying to solve.

Essential to the success of Adanu has been my working partnership with Robert Tornu, our Director of Community Coordination. Early on, he kept validating my vision and direction and even now gives me the courage to keep going. Adanu's success is directly related to his mentoring. He has supported my dreams, seen value in my ideas, and helped me turn them into reality. He understands the role of the communities in establishing constructive, long-term change. Without Robert, this book would never have been published. He says his friendship with me shaped his life; I feel the same about him.

Robert is the face communities associate with Adanu, but he views me as Adanu's leader. The truth is, our collaboration is intertwined and truly started back when we were kids. We love and respect each other highly. I could not imagine Adanu without him and his story is inexorably linked to mine.

After Robert completed sixth grade, his father, an avid advocate for higher education, decided to relocate the family to Ho because of better schooling opportunities. (Previously their home had been in the Kente village of Akpokope.) His mother found housing for them by renting an apartment from my grandmother in Ho. Robert was 12 I was 10.

We became friends immediately. I remember a ritual we had where Robert would take rice, onion, and oil from his mother's kitchen. At that time, he believed she was unaware of this. In retrospect and knowing his mother's kind character, I believe she was well aware he was taking her ration. In any case, Robert and I learned how to make what we called *fried rice*, staying up late into the night far after our parents were asleep. We cooked, ate, and talked long into the night, sometimes as late at 3:00 am, before going to bed.

Time passed. Robert's senior high school years were over and a new chapter had begun in both our lives. Robert started his studies at a teacher's training college while I was still in high school.

After he completed his teacher training, Robert was posted to his first teaching assignment but we stayed in touch. Late one evening during one of his many visits to Ho, he saw me writing on a piece of paper and inquired what I was doing. I told him I was writing a constitution for an organization I was starting. He immediately said he wanted to be a part of it.

How amazing it was that this was just the beginning. We felt so fulfilled in our hearts just thinking about what we could accomplish. These were the days when we had to rotate the use of our only desktop computer while asking our families countless times for help even though we knew they did not believe in what we were doing. They supported our requests because they loved us.

We always reached out to Robert's mother, Fidelia Tornu, and my auntie, Patience Yinkah, for money to

> I knew Richard aspired to create something good with Adanu. He always had a big heart for people in need. As a young man, he would go against his auntie's rules to help friends who needed a place to sleep.
>
> —ROBERT TORNU

implement our programs. For seven years, we utilized a family loan system of borrowing the money from them and repaying them later. My auntie also kindly made her home available to us for hosting and preparing meals for our volunteers.

By the beginning of 2002, I was busy working at the cyber café to earn the money to stay enrolled to study purchasing and supply at the Accra Polytechnic. I officially registered our organization as a Ghanaian non-profit, and we started listing ourselves on different websites to find summer camp volunteers.

The next year brought us many changes, both personally and professionally. Robert married his college girlfriend and started schooling for his adult education diploma at the University of Ghana. I kept plugging away running DIVOG and attending classes. Staying on track with our aspirations did not come easy. While going to school, Robert would squeeze in as much time as he possibly could to visit me at Accra Polytechnic. I remember one of those times vividly.

I was lying in bed while my colleagues were attending lectures. Robert asked, "Why aren't you in class?" I replied, "I'm hungry." I knew that I couldn't focus and grasp what was being taught because of intense hunger. So he took me to the canteen and we ate some rice together. His friendship and belief in my ability to succeed was a big support to me back then, and still is.

Despite the many years of struggle, I was determined to reach my educational goal. Looking back on this memory triggers many emotions for both of us, happiness being the main one. With big dreams and high hopes, we started to make plans to travel to the U.S. for a tech-mission conference. We were very excited because this opportunity promised to equip us with the skills needed to better run our organization.

Procuring our travel visas proved to be the biggest hurdle, but one we were determined to jump over. One of the main documents needed for the visa application was a bank statement.

> The struggle to pay for education is a sad reality in Ghana. But Richard chose to embrace it with determination, always focusing on his goal to higher academics.
>
> —ROBERT TORNU

Thankfully, we had found someone who seemed happy to help us. We were asked to wait outside this guy's hotel to collect the statement from him. We waited and waited long into the night, bitten by mosquitos after we fell asleep near a gutter outside of the hotel. But he never showed up. Eventually, we got what we needed from a friend of a friend, but were still denied the U.S. visa. We pushed this disappointment aside, knowing that we would have many more opportunities to do something similar.

Meanwhile, working at the cyber café, we used any spare moments to promote DIVOG. Sooner than expected, we began to get emails back from people who were willing to come to Ghana and work on two-to-three-week projects. Our first reaction was, "What!??" And that quickly turned into an enthusiastic "WOW!" We had responses from the U.S., Spain, Ireland, and France within the first year. It was incredible. We were very happy to see that kind of interest. Now we had to find out what we were going to do with all those volunteers once they arrived in Ghana.

During this time, a village chief walked into the cyber café to get help with sending an email. He came in with an email message nicely typed out on an A4 piece of paper, sealed in an envelope, with the email address written neatly across the front of the envelope. I had to explain politely to the chief that this was not how email worked. As I opened his envelope and walked him through the email process, I quickly scanned his letter and discovered he was writing it to an organization in The Netherlands to get more funding support for building a school in his community.

While I was reading over the email with him, I started to get excited, thinking, "Wow! This is exactly the kind of community project we want to work for because the community had initiated the project and was already doing its own work!"

As I helped the chief set up his email, I made note of his name, Chief Okuma V, and the name of his community, Kpedze Todze, Ghana, Africa.

I stepped away from him for a few minutes and raced to call Devine. Bursting with enthusiasm, I told him, "You've got to come to the cyber café now! We have to go to this village and see if we can do a project there."

I managed to stall the chief until Devine arrived. We boldly went up to the chief and said, "We want to ask a very big permission from you. We want to come to your village and help you finish your school. The only thing we want is the opportunity to come and build the school with you."

Reminiscing, it makes me smile to think of what Chief Okuma V must have been seeing at that moment: two 22-year-olds working in a cyber café with nothing more than a dream to make life better for other people claiming they could build his school. His pressing need was for a three-classroom junior high school block. After everything I'd been reading about summer camps, I blurted out what sounded to me like the best solution to give to him. I said, "We're going to do a summer camp. We'll bring volunteers to your community and have the community be part of the project."

With no idea of how it would work out, I had the faith that our idea of working in the community could be a better solution for the chief and his village than he would have trying to raise the funding he sought from The Netherlands. It was bizarre that he would have such belief in us and take the risk to trust us with his project. We quickly reached an agreement on the labor, time, and money for materials, and set a time to come to his village to see what they had already done.

However, we chose to make Kpedze-Todze our second project because the chief still wanted to wait until possible funds came in from The Netherlands to move forward with his community's project. For this reason, and because Kpedze-Todze was very remotely located, we waited until the following year to build a three-classroom junior high school there.

Instead, we chose to go to a different community, Amedzofe, because it was closer to Ho and we had volunteers signed up who needed a place to work. This first project came to us through "divine intervention" because it was perfect. That year, Robert and I simply decided that we wanted to go to Amedzofe. Our choice was based mainly on location. Amedzofe was appealing because it was located on the second highest mountain in Ghana, Mount Gemi. Hiking there was popular and the weather was pleasant. Also, due to its proximity near Tati Atome, a monkey sanctuary, and Ote Falls, a beautiful 80-meter waterfall, Amedzofe was a popular tourist destination. We believed we could attract and retain volunteers coming from other parts of the world.

Remotely located, the drive to Amedzofe was a 360km round-trip (246 miles) drive from the Accra airport, the only intercontinental airport in Ghana. Since we had no vehicles to transport volunteers, we were pleased to note that the village was close enough to public transportation to make getting there viable.

With no idea if the chief of Amedzofe needed help, we went to his village, walked up to his house, knocked on his door, and asked him if we could help him build a school in his community. He reply was a simple "yes".

Upon arriving at Amedzofe, we were delighted to see the community was already actively building a three-unit classroom project and recognized the importance of education in their community. We saw all the hard work they had already done and knew that we could complete the project. We had our volunteers and now we had a project!

The community of Amedzofe needed a high school so the students didn't have to attend in Accra, which was way too far away. Sending their children to high school in the faraway city adds costs of transportation, housing, and food. This, coupled with other fees, places a huge financial burden on most families, expenses they simply can't afford.

We brought in a core group of 8-10 volunteers. First, we merely asked our friends to bring along any friends they knew to help us work with the locals. Then, we recruited volunteers through free Internet ads and online job boards like Idealist.org. To our delight, people came from Ireland, the U.S., Spain, and France. The chief from the community found us a nice, vacated home to live in. We did our own cooking. Robert and I rotated meal preparation. We agreed to stay in the village, but we did not want to burden the people, so we brought our own food and made certain that we took care of our own needs.

Before we started, we still had to determine how we were going to set up the summer program and find volunteers to get the work done. We were basically figuring out all this stuff as we went along. Due to prior volunteerism with other non-profits, I had a general idea of what we wanted to do. But in those days, designing a project that included community collaboration was challenging because it was different than anything anyone else was doing.

Soon, we had a large enough group to finish the project, including our first international volunteer, Yen Pham. We had quite an adventure figuring out how to get her from the airport in Accra to the site. One of our local volunteers, Stacy, a friend of ours and a Peace Corps volunteer, was very helpful in making sure Yen Pham connected with us. We were so glad she was patient and arrived in good spirits. Before we knew it, everyone was laying the grounds, erecting the walls for buildings, and getting the work done.

Together, we helped build a three-unit classroom block for the community. Though we didn't raise the funds for this project, we assisted in supporting their endeavors and stayed on an additional six months in the community to train students in computer software applications, such as MS Word, Excel, PowerPoint, and Publisher. We also taught English, Math, and Science. Watching how the community utilized the funds they raised and worked alongside volunteers inspired further development of the Adanu Model. The project placed us in the limelight. With God's guidance, we kept pushing.

We had tremendous fun helping the people! Every day we would dance with the shovels, sing while painting the walls, and feel joy while doing everything that needed to be done to keep the project moving. It was so much fun!

We were doing exactly what I imagined a good community project could be. Our goal was collaboration where everyone involved (volunteers and community members) would participate and experience the result. We wanted the process to be fully transparent and repeatable. Most important, it was imperative that the community knew how to maintain the school after the volunteers left. A sense of commitment and ownership was created in the community due to participation and engagement from the start of the project to its completion. Seeing this model work was exciting.

At the completion of the project, we had a big, colorful ceremony with the chief, other leaders, and the whole community to celebrate the completion of the school. It was such a good day! I was excited to see how we could all come together to build something great. We had created our first school.

Yes, the school building was complete, but success wasn't achieved by the bricks and mortar alone. Initially, the community had to donate money to pay the teachers. When they asked for government funding, the government said no. In the months that followed, a lot of teachers who were teaching elsewhere and wanted the school to succeed volunteered their time to teach. Everyone wanted to see it succeed. Robert trained teachers. An educator myself, I collaborated with him to establish the educational groundwork where students could come to be educated.

When local student test scores began to improve, the government realized that we'd created a viable learning opportunity in Amedzofe. The community then received government support for desks, furniture, and supplies for the school.

We discovered that the people had to help themselves first before the government was ever going to take notice. Once this happened, in two months the school began to attract permanent teachers because the government was willing to pay them. Government's involvement is essential for education to be sustainable because the government provides teachers and teaching supplies. Sustainable success is impossible in Ghana without government participation. It's not easy to start something, but if you have a plan and stay true to your vision, it will succeed.

After all the excitement died down, I stood back for a long time to absorb and understand what had happened and to get clear about why we were doing this work. I started thinking about all the kids who would come through that school and take on their dreams of becoming writers, doctors, lawyers, or anything they wanted to be. Once they got their education, no one could ever take that knowledge or dream away from them. A classroom is one of the most important places for children to see new opportunities for themselves. For us, this was just the beginning of creating the kind of community projects we knew could make a real, significant difference for Ghanaian communities.

As we continued to grow, we helped to build more schools, libraries, water and sanitation facilities, and empowerment centers for women. Our model isn't based on free handouts. Adanu provides a viable, clear path for community members to invest their time, energy, and resources into something that will have a significant impact for generations to come. My soul sang in that realization.

With every completed project, the Adanu team worked and argued harder. This strengthened our brotherhood while reminding us of the importance of the work Adanu was doing. We kept going. Robert and I hosted a medical team from Slovenia and implemented projects in a lot of communities, which caused us both to miss many lectures during the semester, returning to school just in time to complete our end-of-school examinations. I shake my head in amazement, realizing that this was truly the Almighty's plan for our destiny because we passed our exams. One time, I came back and had to write my exam the following day after having worked on a community project. I nailed it. To this day, Robert and I smile about it.

After we had a few great successes, I wanted to keep our organization growing with projects that would inspire my people. I didn't want us to just be another one of those organizations that swoops into a village to set up a water well or build a school without giving the Ghanaian people the tools to maintain and sustain the project on their own. It was important for us to do something different. We wanted to be more engaged with the community in a very focused, intentional way to empower people for generations to come. I knew it was important to capture the innate spirit of joy and collaboration that flows naturally from the Ghanaian people.

In 2006, I completed my tertiary education at Accra Polytechnic and for the next year did my national service in Dzogadze, located about 95km from Ho. All graduates from Ghanaian tertiary institutions must complete a one-year national service. I served while continuing Adanu's work, hosting another team of volunteers, a medical team which showcased another humanitarian layer for Adanu. Again, I went through the same ordeal of jugging multiple obligations, including forgoing lectures so we could travel and be part of the project to provide free healthcare to people in our rural communities.

The following year was our hardest since we only hosted one International volunteer, Tom Gerber, from Switzerland. This setback inspired us to do things differently. I'm pleased to say that we were rewarded for our hard work. In 2006 we successfully secured our first partnership with an international organization, Globe Aware, who ended up securing numerous volunteers for us year after year.

After I finished my national service, Robert got in touch with the headmaster where he was teaching at Tanyigbe Senior High School. The headmaster hired me to teach computer studies. I taught for a year until one day I decided to resign to focus full-time on Adanu. Though Robert was shocked by my decision at the time because he knew full well I needed to earn money to subsidize Adanu's activities and myself, my departure to focus on Adanu changed the future of the organization.

Using every strategy possible to market Adanu's model, my laptop was on 24 hours a day so I could respond immediately to incoming emails. This resulted in recruitment of many more volunteers and, in addition to Globe Aware, landed us an amazing partnership with the Danish organization, MS Global Contact.

Though many people questioned the sensibility of my quitting teaching to focus full-time on Adanu, I knew if I stayed in my comfort zone, I would not make the best use of my time. I had to stretch myself to accomplish what I wanted to do. If I didn't put a lot of work and time into it, my results would not change. Therefore, it was clear to me that I had to make some big concessions and give Adanu the best I had to give. I have never regretted my decision because it completely changed the face of Adanu and kept the dream alive.

By 2009, Robert was a father, husband, and teacher of students at the University of Ghana trying to complete a psychology degree while volunteering his time with Adanu to develop the communities we served. Although working with Adanu was time-consuming, it was also giving him passion and energy. Inspired by my choice to leave paid teaching and take the entrepreneurial step of opening more doors for Adanu, Robert also quit teaching. This was a bold step since teaching had been paying him much better than the stipend he received from Adanu, not to mention the fact he had two children and a wife to support. But he embraced his decision positively, knowing if he worked with Adanu, he could bring us more ideas and support.

"We had a lot of success. And I was happy that I was not teaching in the classroom. I was still working within the school environment to better the lives of children and help them reach their full potential."- Robert Tornu

Adanu's Long-term Impact

Our model takes time but creates permanent change. On May 9, 2017, we had the opportunity to meet with Chief Okusie Akyem Foli V, the chief of Amedzofe, whose community was our first endeavor. We talked with him about our mutual experience and were touched by his memories.

In the 15 years since we created our first school there, he says he's never forgotten Adanu's contribution. I am humbled when he says he's very clear that our work together turned his village into a town. By building their

> **With a book, you send your mind back to remember. To read about what you did here will instill possibility in readers' minds. Everyone will now know you are the people who made us a center for high school education.**
>
> —CHIEF OKUSIE AKYEM FOLI V

school and setting up a computer training program, he says young people now come from all over Ghana to go to high school in Amedzofe. His current dream is to turn the town into a city one day.

Smiling broadly, he told us that to have something written about the work Adanu did for them was a gift and honor. Working with us made a huge difference in his community. Now, people even pay to enroll their kids there because it's such a good school. He told us he hopes the book will inspire other villages to work with us to do what we did in his village.

The chief acknowledged that generations of limited opportunity makes it hard for people to shift their mindset about needing government money to accomplish anything. He told us that in the beginning he nearly ran away when we approached him about beginning a computer education program. He was perplexed by computers and calls himself a BBC (born before computers). He puzzled over how the computer mouse got its name. But patience won out.

Now, because of the program Adanu built, everyone in the community knows about computers and phones. Adanu taught him what could be possible for him and his village. Learning is a gradual process. The Chief says he's still very slow and methodical when using computers. But he says a lot was started by his introduction to Adanu.

> **Adanu merely empowers the community so they can see what they already have and use it to make something happen.**
>
> —CHIEF OKUSIE AKYEM FOLI V

Our conversation reminded me that we must work together with our neighbors. There are things we simply can't do alone. Life itself is a gradual process. It's like preparing rice. First, you must carefully shuck it. Then, you need to boil it. It's gradual, not instantaneous. If you rush the project, you lose. And, if you get to the point where you can't go any further, don't give up. Seek help from your neighbor.

As we were leaving, he warmly shared that the name of his town, Amedzofe, means "human beings from where you originate." He said, "Every human being originated in my village. Thank you for coming home."

CHAPTER THREE

Philanthropic Alignment

The place God calls you to is the place where your
deep gladness and the world's deep hunger meet.

—Frederick Buechner

What happens when philanthropic commitment collides with vision and
purpose?

Shelly and Clint Morse weren't looking for the answer to this question
when they first arrived in Ziavi Adukofe, Ghana in June 2007. But they
would soon discover it on a randomly chosen school intercession project
with their daughter, Julia. Arriving here, they were immediately inspired by
our collaborative model that created long-term relationships with local villages and communities in Ghana. Partnering with Adanu was fully aligned
with their personal ideals:

- All people are created in God's image and worthy of love,
  understanding and friendship.

- Coming alongside others less fortunate and helping them
  reach their potential is a worthy calling.

- It is incumbent upon us to show mercy and love to those who
  are overlooked and unnoticed.

- Good stewardship means giving to work being done with
  thoughtful strategies to restore justice.

- Shelly and Clint know they can't help every person in need. But
  they were inspired to help wherever and whenever they could.
  They fell in love with the warm-hearted, sincere Ghanaian people.

> ❝ At Adanu, we found passionate, selfless people who were committed to doing the work needed to be done to help their communities. ❞
>
> —SHELLY MORSE

With these ideals deeply embedded in their decision to help, Shelly and Clint decided to assist Adanu in our funding and in building a stronger business model. The underlying love and alliance between The Mosaic Company (their company) and Adanu would flourish beyond anything they, or we, could possibly imagine.

In the ten years we have known them they have become business advisors providing mentoring and advice and funded 13 school buildings as well as numerous other projects such as water projects, sanitation blocks, libraries and even a pickleball court.

Through our partnership with the Morses, in 2013 we started a registered 501(c)3 (non-profit) organization in the U.S.A. to support our work. Currently, it is named Friends of Adanu.

Then, in 2014, we re-branded and renamed our organization to Adanu (www.adanu.org). The name DIVOG had been a good one, but it confused people about what we were doing. We needed a clearer message. In the Ewe language, which is the language spoken by the people of the Volta Region of Ghana, Adanu means, "wise collaboration." It was perfect for what we wanted to represent: Ghanaian culture, community, collaboration, sustainment, inspiration, empowerment, and partnership. Adanu became the perfect name to capture the kind of work we were committed to doing throughout Ghana.

Today, Shelly is our mentor, board member, and financial partner. But we also call her "Mama" because the bond between us is that great. Life has been fortunate to her and she's been able to support us in many ways. But we always know, there's no promises in life. God gives so that she can give. Should that change for any reason, we are still bonded forever through our deep love for the work we do, and each other. Building lasting connections is the cornerstone of Adanu.

The Mosaic Company—Corporate Volunteerism

As the founder of The Mosaic Company, a Seattle-based energy consulting firm, Clint realized that Adanu aligned well with his own leadership and business ideals. He believes that serving others is the foundation for success in business and in life, and that true collaboration and respect for others makes all the difference. Adanu has been a rich environment for Mosaic employees to volunteer and learn to use collaboration to look for ways to accomplish a job and serve their clients well.

Mosaic works with Adanu as a partner in the same manner Adanu collaborates with individual Ghanaian communities. Each partner brings what resources they can to the project, all with a goal to help the other become self-sustaining. Adanu supports the community in decision-making and identifying community resources and leaders, while also helping to connect the community with outside resources, such as Mosaic employees, who provide their expertise and support.

Adanu provides an opportunity for other corporate partners to carry out their philanthropic missions and provide employees with rich experiences. Though funding is always welcome, partnering with us is not limited to financial support. Western volunteers traveling to Ghana are a key aspect of our success. Volunteers, simply by their presence, expertise, and hard work helps enable Ghanaians to improve their lives and communities.

Volunteers return home knowing their experience with Adanu changed them. Often, they are inspired to reach out in their own communities to engage in activities that expand Adanu's reach, albeit often in invisible ways.

Through the years, corporate volunteers have played an important part in Adana. Their stories illuminate the wonderful experiences volunteers have when they come to Ghana.

Miranda Leurquin, Mosaic's Executive Vice President of People Operations, was 28 years old in 2008 when she was chosen through an anonymous application process to travel to Ghana to work with Adanu to help improve the school structures at Ziave-Adukope. That inaugural trip has since evolved into an ongoing partnership that continues to link Adanu and Mosaic. Miranda has since returned four times. She said to me that she had an immediate connection with the community the minute she arrived.

Miranda's Story

That first night I was fumbling through the woods to find a place with a little bit of privacy to relieve myself in the bushes about 200 feet away from the hut, headed basically into the wilderness. A couple of community members saw me fumbling, trying to figure out where I was going. The next thing I knew, I had a child holding my hand, guiding me through the dark. And it was just like that every single moment of the trip.

Seeing a typical Ghanaian elementary classroom for the first time was a bit shocking. Countless students were gathered under a mango tree, while their teacher half-heartedly presented the lesson. Chickens and goats wandered through the fidgeting group, and parents periodically summoned a son or daughter in the middle of the day to return home to help with the family farm. On occasion, snakes dropped from a tree, and the bugs, heat, and passing community members often drew students' attention from the lesson at hand. The teachers, uninspired and with few resources, sometimes arrived unprepared, or didn't show up at all.

I could see the kids were distracted and that it wasn't a good environment for anybody. It was frustrating for the teachers too because it was difficult to compete against all the distractions vying for the kids' attention.

I've been to Ghana several times and have witnessed a profound change over the years because of all the different pieces working together. Having the school buildings, just those walls, makes an incredible difference for the kids. It also attracts quality teachers. Teachers are proud to work in a new school building so they put forth a sincere effort to provide kids with a good education.

I have especially enjoyed returning and reconnecting with students. The element of personal connection and engagement seems central to the success of Adanu's approach, which is a commitment to building and maintaining relationships.

From my perspective as a human resources leader at Mosaic,

another benefit of these trips is the working relationship of the company's co-workers who travel together, growing both trust and friendship as they work for a common goal. Our company's clients find merit in this as well. They love to hear about the work Mosaic is doing in Ghana, even though they aren't necessarily going themselves. The stories we tell are inspiring. Clients think it's awesome that, as an employer, Mosaic would support employees to volunteer their time and energy in Ghana to help others. Some clients and their families have even gone on our trips!

The relationship with Adanu brings a lot of different benefits to companies. The collaboration is a boon to their recruiting, particularly with talented, younger employees. Employer support for community service and community involvement has become increasingly important to employees over the years. Over 90 percent of Mosaic's candidates ask what the company is doing from a community standpoint. In my role with human resources, I encourage our recruiting team to share the company's work with Adanu to help us attract strong talent.

The true impetus for Mosaic's support of volunteer work is the company's alignment with Adanu's mission of helping these Ghanaian communities help themselves.

Iris' Story

When Iris Lemmer, a Mosaic employee, volunteered with Adanu at Hehekpoe, she gained an appreciation for how important something as fundamental as fresh water is to villages here. In a post on Adanu's website she wrote that part of her immersive experience was to go to the nearby pond and carry a pail of water on her head for a few blocks to where it was needed. The women in the village have been doing that task their whole lives. She said she had to cheat and hold on with her hands to keep the water bucket on her head. She got a good upper arm workout that day.

Iris also helped mix and mold cement blocks for the foundation of a new water system Adanu constructed for the primary school. It was grueling but gratifying work. Upon completion the entire village turned out to celebrate. A parade of women carrying beautiful Ghanaian fabrics on their heads in large bowls, people in traditional garb and a group of bongo and conga drummers performing traditional music started the festivities, which lasted all night. Elders spoke to the volunteers and the whole community, thanking everyone for the work they'd done to make the project a success. Many speeches and words of gratitude were exchanged between villagers and the team. After more dancing and drumming, a ceremonial ribbon was cut to open the water system. As villagers watched water come out of the tank's spigot, people of all ages cheered with delight. Big cheers, enthusiastic drumming, ecstatic dancing, and a massive bonfire followed.

Built on these personal connections, corporate volunteerism in Ghanaian communities continues to grow. Regarding the key ingredient that makes these collaborations work, Don Davis, a technology specialist who has gone to Ghana three times on company volunteer trips, also described the sense of heart and community-mindedness he feels when he visits.

Don has a wonderful, generous spirit that he shares openly with other volunteers. He often will bring everyone together for dinner, making sure no one is left out.

I asked him to tell me about an event that he remembers most vividly, and he told me about the first night of his second visit.

What an amazing experience to see an entire village of people come together to celebrate water coming out of a spigot! I'm not sure I can express the joy of what I experienced. Our team all watched in amazement as dancing and celebration continued for hours. We all realized that much like in our own culture, this was a time for young adults to dance close with one another. You could see little budding romances happening all over the place. I guess teenage anxiety is typical in all cultures. I'll never forget this experience. It will stay in my heart forever.

—IRIS LEMMER

Don's Story

As I lay in a bed in a home that a family had vacated to give me and another volunteer a place to live for a week, I was falling asleep in the dark to the sound of drummers practicing in the village at night. I was struck by how village members share everything. They don't have fences. Very few people have formal houses. Most live in clapboard huts with thatched roofs. Some places don't even have walls. There's limited commerce going back and forth. One family goes to the market and they pick up the okra and eggplants. Another specializes in getting fish. Yet another harvests corn in the fields nearby. The rural villages are communal with their own micro-economy.

It was powerful, too, to grasp that the people in rural Ghana do pretty much the same thing as people in downtown Seattle do on any given day of the week. They get up, take a shower, eat breakfast, and go to work. Essentially, it's very much the same in Los Angeles or Seattle as it is in Ghana. It's just the environment that is different.

Being in Ghana helped me reconsider the power of community in my own life and how I might become generous and expand my capacity for sharing. I had an epiphany to be more intentional about connecting with my own family. I was concerned that doing so might negatively impact my performance at work. The strange part was I discovered that by focusing more on my family I became more productive and engaged at work than I'd been at any point in my professional life. I thought less about deliverables and deadlines and gave attention to more qualitative things, such as how my coworkers were doing and how I could help them. And in spite of this, the quality and timeliness of my work production became better than ever.

There's a rich, deep perspective you develop by volunteering with co-workers in Ghana. The experience helps you better understand your colleagues, your customers, and challenges they face.

Don's volunteer experience echoes the benefits Miranda has seen from those who have brought the best of the Ghanaian community spirit back to their offices.

Heidi's Story

Volunteer Heidi Scott echoed this sentiment when she talked to me about a transformational experience she had during her visit to Ghana. She said she befriended a woman named Agnes who invited her into her home to learn how to make a traditional meal. She sat with Agnes by an open fire hearth, watching her chop and prepare the food while telling Heidi about her life.

On the evening before a group departs a village, there is often a final ceremony and celebration as a way to thank the volunteers. Stories volunteers tell demonstrate how this collaboration between volunteers and Ghanaians helps to support their communities beyond the building of schools and other projects. The relationships made during this time and the benefit of this immersive experience for both Ghanaians and volunteers are profound and substantial.

I saw such grit and gentleness in Agnes. Talk about a strong woman! The cool thing was that the next evening she found me at the bonfire and taught me to dance. The following morning when our team was preparing to leave, she asked me to walk back to her home so I could say goodbye to her family. It was a special time to hug and declare our friendship. I hope to see her again and encourage her in her life."

—HEIDI SCOTT

Ryan's Story

Ryan Aller remembers sitting down with his two sons, Noah and Nathan, to tell them he would be traveling to Ghana to help finish the construction of a library at Hehekpoe. He told them the library needed books so his sons decided to donate some of theirs. They ended up packing over 70 pounds of books for him to take and donate to the new library. Some of these books were his boys' favorites.

When Ryan arrived in Hehekpoe and visited the new library he saw all the donated books had already been placed on the shelves. He looked through the books until he came to a familiar one that he had read many times to his boys.

There were a few children from the village sitting on the porch of the library, so Ryan decided he would read the book aloud one more time before leaving it in Ghana for those children to enjoy. Halfway through his reading of the book, he noticed that the number of children had increased, and they were all standing around him and listening to the story of *Fly Guy*. Some were listening, others repeating, and some were reading along. It was a special moment for him.

When he returned home, Ryan showed a video of him reading the book to the children in Hehekpoe to his boys. Both boys beamed with huge smiles. They were happy to see the items they had donated being enjoyed by so many children.

Far-reaching influence of volunteers

When volunteers return home, their commitment to helping empower Ghanaian communities usually continues in amazing ways. They often reach out to their friends to share about the experience and to spread the word about Adanu's model of community development. It's been amazing to experience the generosity of our philanthropic partners.

The ongoing collaboration between Adanu, Ghanaian communities, volunteers, and donors has resulted in multiple schools, urinals, libraries, playgrounds, and numerous other projects region-wide in about 55 communities in the Volta region.

Partnerships with Organizations

Adanu actively seeks corporate partnerships. Our model relies on establishing collaborative relationships outside of Ghana. Volunteers contribute the vital resources of hope and opportunity. By giving to Adanu, companies of all sizes have the opportunity to achieve their philanthropic and social responsibility goals, as well as build strong employee teamwork, camaraderie and lasting friendships through volunteering in Ghana.

We have led organizations and universities to understand the Adanu model, and eventually to partner with us in promoting sustainable development. We invite you to consider partnership and participation with us. Together, sustainable change is possible.

Recently we've received the following recognition:

Coca Cola Young Achiever

In early 2017, to mark Ghana's 60th Independence Day anniversary, Coca-Cola launched a campaign, *Ghana's 60th,* that sought to celebrate 60 exceptional Ghanaians who are trailblazers and have been inspirational to the communities in Ghana. The object of the campaign was to celebrate young achievers, give them a platform to showcase their passion for what they do, and remind Ghanaians that the country is full of opportunities for anyone willing to explore them.

A media call went out looking for nominations to celebrate the achievements in the fields of Education, Entrepreneurship, Entertainment/Media, Health, Sports and Technology. With over 2,000 nominees, response from the public was overwhelming. Representing Adanu, I was proud to receive the award as the Coca-Cola Young Achiever in the Education category.

The Education Community Award
for Best Education Partnership in Ghana

2017 was a big year for Adanu. Neogenics Education, Ghana/UK named us Best Education Partnership in Ghana with one of the Education Community (EDUCOM) Awards. The Education Partnership Category focuses on community partnership, collaboration, and engagement in education. The award is an inspiration for all of us at Adanu as we continue to work collaboratively with our communities. We might not have all the solutions to Ghana's problem, but in our small way we will continue to engage and partner with all stakeholders in supporting the change we want to see in our various communities through education. I feel blessed.

adanu

Photo album

Mypa Buckner, Adanu's Director of Operations, pours through applications that we receive from villages throughout Ghana. The need is great!

Richard connecting with a few of the children we meet while scouting remote villages, hoping to guide them to a brighter future.

As part of Adanu's community assessment, Robert explains the process to community leaders, teachers, and moms and dads from the village.

45

Standing to their feet to greet us, as we
tour their school, these students hope that
our presence signals help for a better life.

Human connection is the
immeasurable gift we all
receive and give. Every child
deserves a proper education.

A typical
fourth-
grade class
persevering
to learn in
spite of no
classroom or
textbooks,
a common
scene in
villages
throughout
Ghana.

Young students huddle together as they wait out a sudden downpour.
Rain is a constant interference for students in rural villages.

Our visit has become a big distraction to these little ones. Learning without
classrooms makes teaching difficult and learning nearly impossible.

While most villages have no place for students to relieve
themselves privately, this structure will be replaced by a new
urinal that is sanitary and provides better privacy.

This completed urinal is a typical project done on volunteer trips. It is a first step in assessing community commitment and involvement, both requirements for building a school.

Queen Mother Bernice breaks ground for the upcoming 1-6 grade school building, a continuation of our partnership in Hehekpoe.

Hoping for a way up for their daughters, women work alongside men, adding to a day that is already filled with physical labor.

A Brightlight volunteer lays brick for a urinal project. The collaboration between the village mason and the young volunteer is what we long to see.

Young, old, male, female, African, westerner—it truly takes a village.

This school has been a labor of love. The beautiful artwork was provided by our creative volunteers.

49

Everyone gathers to celebrate the successful completion of another Adanu project. For most villagers, a classroom is something they only dream of. This village has seen their dream come true.

Every morning and evening the women and children fetch water for their families. The community's only water source, this pond is contaminated and shared with animals, used for bathing and laundry.

Angelbert Ankah, Director of Construction, measures the base for a new water tank. He will spend the time needed mentoring locals about the ins and outs of various construction projects.

Rubbing shoulders with the locals, Adanu volunteers carry hand-molded bricks to a place where they are left to dry.

These young students FINALLY can enjoy clean water! This tank project will provide the school with clean drinking water and a way for children to wash their hands and prevent the spread of disease. Students no longer have to miss valuable classroom time walking to fetch water.

Luci Sanchez leads a class on hand washing and germs in conjunction with the water tank project, an example of western volunteers demonstrating to village teachers the importance of student participation in their learning. Making learning fun and interactive is a new concept for most.

Kindergarteners enjoying lunch as part of the Hehekpoe PTA program. Parents volunteer in teams to provide a hot, nutritious lunch once a week.

The new school garden planted by students is producing healthy greens. Moms were shown how to cook these cocoa yam leaves and add them to the PTA's lunch program diet.

The daily chore of sweeping the school grounds is done by every student, every morning.

A young girl begins the long trek to her family's farm. As part of her daily responsibility, she will return with a heavy load of produce. Education offers her an opportunity to move beyond a future of subsistence farming.

A little table and stool carried from home will serve as a school desk and chair today.

Luvudo kindergarteners pose to show appreciation for their new school. Little do these young minds know how this classroom will impact their lives.

It's tough say good-bye. Lives are forever changed by this shared experience.

While volunteers leave the village for a day of sight-seeing, community members continue working on their own. This affords Adanu an opportunity to assess and measure community commitment.

A job well done.

Everyone loves a new kindergarten class room.

Some of Adanu's brightest success stories with Shelly Morse. These young adults were children when Adanu began work in their villages. Now, they are an HR manager, a journalist, a reporter, an insurance broker, a science teacher, a nurse, and the manager of a pharmaceutical company. All of them speak of the impact volunteers made in their young lives, second to the importance of attending class in a school building.

Don Davis, an Adanu volunteer, shares technology with a throng of eager learners. Children are longing for an opportunity to explore life beyond their village.

This music wall has served two purposes: kindergarteners had hours of fun, and volunteers demonstrated how something wonderful can be made from the ordinary things available within the village.

Adanu volunteers, John Benoit and Clint Morse, work after hours on the kindergarten playground.

A visit to the local market for supplies and now an opportunity to prepare a meal with a family. This is a part of Adanu's immersive volunteer experience.

Excited by the changes, community members proudly erect a sign on a nearby highway to share the Adanu/Hehekpoe story with all who drive by.

Rachel Collier, an Adanu volunteer, enjoys the monkey sanctuary while taking a break from volunteering in the village. The Tafi Atome Monkey Sanctuary is one of the many stops volunteers visit while in the Volta Region.

These volunteers have been lavished with beautiful Ghanaian clothing and beads by their host family. Next stop is Sunday worship.

Miranda Leurquin, an Adanu board member, is given a dancing lesson by her friend. Even the youngest are eager to teach local dance to visitors.

The ladies of Woadze Tsatoe hand carved these designs into blocks they will use to create beautiful batik fabrics. This new business initiated by NYU Stern School of Business students is bringing much needed opportunity. Once a thriving fishing community, the lake they live near has been over-fished and no longer provides a useful livelihood.

Volunteers are given the unique opportunity of learning how Ghanaians make their one-of-a-kind batik cloth.

NYU Stern School of Business students celebrating the new batik business they've worked tirelessly to help the community create. Families will now have income to support their children's educational needs.

Inspired by the commitment and passion he saw in Luvudo, volunteer Todd Lotzer returned home and raised the money to financially support the building of a library. Having learned how to come together on previous projects, community members are now able to tackle this project on their own.

These courageous ladies are forming adult literacy groups in their communities. They desperately want to learn English, which will prevent them from being taken advantage of while selling their goods at the market, and help them be involved in their children's education. Ultimately, this accomplishment brings dignity and self-respect.

Because of Global Hope Alliance's partnership with ADANU, this young girl has a new friend she can share life with outside of her remote village. Surely both will be enlightened by the correspondence.

We are so grateful to Kokanee Elementary and other partners for caring so much. The library was filled with books for the children to enjoy and they are also serving as learning materials for the adult literacy program.

Joanne Provo enjoys the library with her young friends. She and her friends financed this library as a birthday gift to herself.

Adanu volunteer, Iris Lemmer, reads one of the donated books to a group of kids at the new library at Luvudo. They are eager to grasp what these pages offer.

Richard and Robert return to say thank you to the chief of the first village they worked in with volunteers. He believed in them and their dream for rural villages. Togbe Okusie Akyem-foli V of the Amedzofi village credits Adanu, "We are no longer an overlooked village. Now, 14 years later, we are a vibrant town with excellent educational standards for all students."

Happy to be a family and team! After a long day of strategic planning and team building, an evening river cruise is on the agenda!

"We face neither east nor west. We face forward."
—Dr. Kwame Nkrumah
(Ghana's first president)

Clint and Julia Morse draw a crowd while building a
school desk on their first trip to Ghana in 2008.

PART II

Community Profiles

Adanu works with many communities in Ghana. For the purposes of this book, we will focus on three where we've built long and extensive relationships: Hehekpoe, Luvudo, and Kpedze-Todze.

If you're curious about the locations of these communities and others where Adanu has worked, please scan this QR code that will take you to an Adanu app. Then, click on Find a Village.

CHAPTER FOUR

Hehekpoe (The HAPPI Project)

Everyone in Hehekpoe wakes at dawn. Since there is no running water, women and children fetch water in an open, polluted pond shared with local cattle. The men go to work on their farms, often 2-3 miles away, travelling by foot, without breakfast. Once there, they prepare roasted cassava (a root vegetable) or maize (corn).

Children start early on house chores, sweeping, cleaning, and making breakfast, often working for up to two hours before going to school. Breakfasts are large in Hehekpoe because it is the only meal until dinner. Once the kids are sent off to school, the women—many with infants wrapped on their backs—either join the men at the farm or walk several miles to the closest markets to sell produce so they can buy farm equipment or household items. After a long day, the adults have the same long walk home, often carrying firewood or produce on their heads. Although Hehekpoe has electricity, there is limited access and little money for it, so the day ends early and night comes quickly.

Linked together by five villages, Kpordoave, Meyikpor, Dorkpo, Kperkpoe, and Tevikpoe, with a total population of over 1,000 people, Hehekpoe's major occupation is cassava and maize farming, but community members also raise goats, cattle and chickens. However, despite being successful farmers, the local market is too far away to easily sell most of their produce, making farming more a subsistence crop than a lucrative one. Healthcare is also limited, the closet clinic is several miles away and there are no doctors living in the community.

In the 1977–1978 academic year, the Salvation Army facilitated construction of two K-6 school buildings in Hehekpoe, funded by the government, each with three classrooms. These buildings have roofs but no walls or attached doors and windows and because of the number of students many classes are still held under trees. Weather conditions, goats, chickens and other distractions are constant. Classrooms lack furniture. Currently eight trained and nine untrained teachers share five desks. Students share desks and the youngest carry them from home. Children must travel five miles to the nearby town of Kpetsu if they want to use a computer. Hehekpoe also has a crumbling, dilapidated junior high school structure with similar conditions.

Hehekpoe was a community ripe for our help. After going through our extensive selection and assessment process in 2012, Hehekpoe was selected for a test project. Adanu agreed to construct a urinal, using the Adanu Model to access the community's commitment and readiness for construction of a new Kindergarten block. The urinal was a huge success, so we moved forward to build a new kindergarten that included two classrooms, an activity/nap room, flush toilets and shower, an office, playground, and school garden.

Following Adanu's Model, the community agreed to provide land, masons, carpenters, steel benders, and other skilled and unskilled labor. Parents were also asked to provide contributions for their children's uniforms and school supplies. We were gaining momentum and exicitement was growing in the village, but in our hearts as well.

Schools in these villages are built the old-fashioned way. We don't use modern-day equipment like bull-dozers, cranes, and power saws. Communities clear the land using shovels, pick axes, head pans for carrying water, and other hand tools. Women fetch water from the nearest river throughout the construction. They mix sand and cement with water by hand to form the over 3,000 bricks needed for a building. The entire construction project is labor-intensive, both in skilled and unskilled labor. The whole community helps on the project, from pouring the foundation of the building to placing every brick. Carpenters build doors, windows, and roofs. The masons, carpenters, steel benders, and painters all work collaboratively to ensure the work is done properly, and to the highest quality.

Construction on the kindergarten block took about 3 months. Since the community members are farmers, they put themselves into rotating groups so that they could limit the number of days each community member would need to participate. They need to be able to continue farming as much as possible, so they don't lose their crops. Everyone works extremely hard to balance their day-to-day responsibilities with the work required on the school.

Adanu also contacted Hehekpoe leaders who had outside resources, including instructional support from the District Education Directorate in Adaklu District and the Salvation Army Regional Education Unit in the nearby village of Ho. The project was also supported by contributions from a member of Parliament.

The kindergarten block project was wildly successful. It has been touted as the nicest kindergarten in all of the Volta region due to the school garden, water tank, flush toilets/showers, activity/nap room, and beautiful painted and appointed class rooms. Schools in Ghana are nothing like schools in America so it can be hard to explain how profound an impact something as simple as a brightly-lit, clean room can have on learning.

Their enthusiasm for what they had accomplished prompted Hehekpoe to approach Adanu in 2014 to pursue another project, a water catchment tank for the school (completed in 2015).

Hehekpoe-Adanu-Pilot-Project-Initiative (HAPPI)

Community members were so engaged and supportive of each other and the Adanu model, that we decided to partner with Hehekpoe in a pilot project to measure and document successful educational improvements to determine and demonstrate how our process works and the positive outcomes we are able to achieve. The program commits Adanu resources to the school to track outcomes over several years, for both students and the community. We've seen a lot of positive impact from it already, not only on the students, but also in the community.

As an example, starting with the cohort of kindergarteners in the 2012 academic year, student academic scores are being compiled and compared to previous cohorts in an attempt to link directly the impact of our community development model. Our hope is that we will be able to quantitatively demonstrate the results of the "wise collaboration" the Adanu Model is able to produce, and show the change communities are experiencing.

Volunteers Make a Difference

We've had countless special experiences with volunteers in Hehekpoe. One memorable afternoon we gathered the community together around a new water tank that had been erected to provide clean water for the kindergarten. Volunteer Luci Sanchez came to Ghana with a lesson for the kids on germs. She taught the entire community how to wash their hands and remove the germs and how hygiene would improve health in the school. After squirting glitter gel on the kids' hands, she instructed the kids on proper hand-washing. They gathered in lines next to the hand-washing stations, excited to get a chance to both put glitter on their hands and to see if they could remove it. Scrubbing briskly, the glitter was everywhere. Before long, parents, chiefs, and elders were lining up to remove the "germs". Everyone was giggling as they struggled to get clean while learning an important lesson.

Partnering with the Hehekpoe Parent Teacher Association

Adanu helped the parents at Hehekpoe start their first PTA, and they have gotten busy, including starting a school lunch program, acquiring new instructional materials, building a school garden, and providing books and school uniforms for children whose parents can't afford them.

A school lunch program was a new idea because most students don't eat lunch. However, with hungry kids, particularly young ones, trying to learn the alphabet, numbers, and colors, attention spans can become very short.

The lunch program has been a great success. Four to five parents sign up to buy and cook one lunch for all the kindergarten kids one day a week. The parents rotate this responsibility. The PTA is looking to expand the lunch program to other days during the week. Right now, it's not a fully sustainable program because parents with limited resources are not be able to afford lunches for the children every day. The cost is eight cents per day for each child. The cost to feed lunch to the entire school costs about 50 dollars per week. But the community has not let this deter them. In April 2016, with the help of volunteers, a school garden was built located close to the school. Each class is responsible for planting a specific crop, which will be harvested and used in the lunch program, with any extra being sold to the community to raise money for school operations and building upkeep. This is a sustainable solution that was originated by the creativity and passion of the community.

On a trip in the fall of 2016, Shelly, Karen, and Betsy Benoit volunteered in the Hehekpoe community. Followed by a group of very curious, observant kids eager to help, they all moseyed into the garden to pick cocoa yam leaves to prepare an all-school lunch that day. Between them, they only had one dull machete. So, while there wasn't much opportunity for the kids to help, the three of them hacked away at the leaves which had been planted by students earlier that spring. Bundling the greens in their arms, they headed back to the outdoor school kitchen. They tossed the leaves into a large pot and cooked them with oil, garlic and a delicious, salty, cumin-flavored spice. The result was magnificent! It was so good that the kids requested it be added to what they usually eat at school. When they went home, they even asked their parents to make it for dinner.

Here are some highlights resulting from the community of Hohekpoe's partnership with Adanu:

- We have completed the kindergarten and are in the process of building new classrooms for elementary students, grades 1-6. These teachers and students will have the opportunity to learn in classrooms with beautifully painted walls, chalkboards, a weatherproof roof, and electricity to power ceiling fans.

- There is a new, heavily used library that includes many books donated by Mosaic employees, Alma College, Literacy Beyond Borders, and others.

- We helped construct a urinal and build two playgrounds, and we conducted teacher trainings, implemented handwashing stations, and helped form a vibrant PTA, all of which serve a growing student population.

- Since the beginning of HAPPI, enrollment has increased by 31%. Families see greater value in educating their children and the students are excited about going to school. And metrics are in place to measure academic improvement, graduation rates, and other quantitative benefits.

Words of the Chief

As leader of the Hehekpoe community, Chief Keti Mawusi said that although the Salvation Army had built schools in 1977 and said they planned to send someone to manage the school, no follow-up was provided. Local children were getting bored and dropping out of school. For the first time, children are enthused about learning.

The Chief says that since Adanu came, the children are more interested in learning to read. They're seen walking around reciting their ABCs. There has been a lot of change through having the library, too. Kids want to come back for two more hours in the evening to study at the library. Parents find this very encouraging.

In the past, children here were often taken out of school, as parents saw schooling as a waste of time. It's different now. The new buildings have fostered the environment where the value of school is evident so more parents are supporting their kids. Young people from other communities are even coming to Hehekpoe to go to school. They feel the fever! The seeds for being a district model have been planted.

It is Adanu's dream to make Hehekpoe a shining community and a model for other communities across Ghana. When we emphasize the need for every child to go to school, people now understand and see the benefit. And our children will grow up with greater opportunity.

Words of the Queen Mother

Queen Mother Bernice Asigbey agrees that working with Adanu has strengthened the community. She told me there's a growing spirit of coming together for a common goal. People know education will bring opportunity and benefit to their lives.

Though not originally from Hehekpoe, Bernice came here in 1982 when she married her husband. In the years that followed, she became highly committed to serving the needs of women in the community. Speaking for them when they needed their concerns known to the chiefs and elders, she became "the face of the women in the community," eventually being named Queen Mother by the other women. She expresses her service heart to the community and they respond. She says it's an honor to serve her village.

A mother of three children, 12, 13, and 21 years old, Bernice knows the value of education for children and realizes how working together for that common goal builds community. Before Adanu came to Hehekpoe, she remembers it was very quiet there and farming was the focus of life. People were unwilling to pull together for a common purpose. Respect for elders was lacking. Kids were getting in trouble with the police. Few cared about the good of the community. They were only concerned about themselves. She has noticed that since working with Adanu, the mindset of the whole community has changed.

People are coming together for community work and they're engaged in large numbers. When the women carry water or the men pour concrete, a building is built. They see the results of their labor and feel community spirit. Years ago, building a school or library would not have happened. Now, the library is a big part of the community. People like that their kids use it and see how education will bring opportunity. It's an alternative to farming. There is hope that every educated child will grow up and bring back the benefits of their education to the community at large.

She equates the Adanu Model to the Golden Rule and the Christian life of loving your neighbor as yourself. Families in the community are learning to share their homes and give their love openly.

The Queen Mother says that she wants women of the world to be a part of every opportunity, and that girls' education is very important. Women view the education of their children as a high priority. Her view is that all things women are part of become more successful than male only initiatives. The entire community is elevated when women are viewed as leaders. She prays that Adanu will be blessed abundantly.

Words of a Mother

Prior to Adanu, Ruth Ayim's fourth-grade son had to attend a sixth-grade class because there was no fourth-grade classes. Developmentally, this was very difficult for him because he wasn't being taught the right information or way for a child of his age, she wasn't inspired to send him to school.

But due to Adanu, she's noticed a big difference with her younger daughter, Madelaine. Her education has been age-appropriate and she started

> **❝**Madelaine is having a much different experience since Adanu built the school. I've seen a big shift in attitude. She's lucky. The first thing my daughter does when she gets home is change into her home clothes and start her homework. I make sure the kids are doing their homework together. Madelaine's education is helping the entire family. Our foundation as a family is stronger now. My kids are eager to read. In the past, this wasn't the norm in my family or the community. Every child now attempts to read. Every parent should send their children to school because education holds the key to development. Parents need to realize their kids will one day be Ghana's leaders and that will benefit them as parents.**❞**

—RUTH AYIM

kindergarten attending class in the new school building. She's excelling. Madelaine began her education when we started the HAPPI project. While she's being taught, she isn't distracted by weather, animals and the other activities in the village that her siblings experienced. She's already starting school with a stronger foundation than they did.

Ruth has seen a transformation in the community. Before Adanu came to Hehekpoe, people were apathetic about getting involved. Now they're working toward a common goal. She sees a tremendous shift in people's "call to duty." She thanks the Adanu team and Almighty God for her good fortune.

Words of a Teacher

Mr. Viktor Gameli, a kindergarten teacher, attests to the poor conditions faced in the village school before Adanu came to their community. Before Adanu helped build the kindergarten, Viktor taught classes under a tree. Typical of so many communities in Ghana, he was teaching outdoors and his students, particularly the younger ones, were distracted by animals and noises. Wet, muddy conditions during rainstorms meant he often had to cancel school. He had no teaching materials. Kids had small, slate hand-held chalkboards to work on. Children had to carry chairs on their heads from home to the school classroom. The cost of school supplies often resulted in parents pulling their kids out of school. Academic achievement and interest were low.

Viktor said, "I feel more credible teaching in a school building instead of under a tree. Now I can genuinely teach. Students have educational materials to interest them. They can develop their ideas better, and at a higher level. They are happier than they were in the past. Before, they never knew if their classroom would be shut down by weather conditions which was very discouraging for both me and them. Now they are so motivated they get to school before I do."

> Students' improved attitudes are influencing adults to get involved in supporting the school. The parents see their kids' characters changing in a positive way, and they like to observe students reciting poetry and showing a desire to learn. Improved education improves many aspects of the whole community.
>
> —VICTOR GAMELI

The school structure in Hehekpoe is attracting children from far away villages to learn because they have age-appropriate storybooks, drawing materials, curriculum, games, and even a nap room with mats for the young students. Higher enrollment has helped the school provide education to more people. The increased enrollment captured the government's attention, resulting in even more educational materials being provided for the school. Because the government is providing more and better materials, teachers want to be placed there. Every aspect of the program is being elevated.

Words of a Librarian

Robert Dzehe teaches first through seventh grade in Hehekpoe during the day, and volunteers two hours every weeknight at the Hehekpoe library.

When Robert was nine years old, he was sent to live with his aunt in an urban area to go to school. Gone from Hehekpoe for eleven years, he says it wasn't a bad experience because at least he was living with family. But when he returned to teach in Hehekpoe, he was surprised to discover the low level of reading ability among his peers and other children in his community.

Alongside Adanu volunteers, he was excited to set up the library. Classes meet twice a week in the library with their teachers. To help in the evenings, the older kids come in at the same time as the younger ones. Sometimes they try to tell the story by looking at the pictures because they don't always want to read, but they're improving.

Robert appreciates the Adanu model because he has witnessed first-hand that every contribution given benefits a community. The resources of time, talents, and financial support are always put to optimal use in the village.

Many kids have gone from disliking books to viewing reading as a hobby. Reading is important because it helps everyone learn to communicate with people around the world and fit in globally.

The library is primarily used by the children, but I'd like to share the value of the library with adults by offering them a literacy program. Most adults in Hehekpoe don't know how to read, so they stay away from the library.

Often, Hehekpoe women who don't speak English are exploited in the market by less-than-honest buyers who do. Speaking English protects women from this manipulation and empowers them in an everyday way. With an education, you have the key to climb higher. When a village in the region has a library, the literacy rate increases too.

English is a national language. Children start learning it in kindergarten and use it fulltime starting in the 4th grade. This is one reason it is so important for kindergarten through third grade to be given a strong foundation in English. Plus, when kids are with their friends and they're all speaking and studying English, everyone learns. —ROBERT DZEHE

When asked why Westerners should care if Ghanaian children are literate, Robert agrees with me that it is crucial for their success. Years from now, children of today will be the leaders in the government and will make decisions that affect the world and bring about the changes most needed in Ghana. Investing in these children means they will be educated so that they can come up with creative solutions and make thoughtful decisions.

Robert also appreciates the volunteer aspect of Adanu's model. He said villagers remember when volunteers come to their community, and that it influences children to want to learn. Community members never forget what a difference volunteers make in their lives.

A Model for Metrics

Adanu is partnering with Hehekpoe to create a model for metrics measurement to document the improvements we are gaining. We will use this data to improve what is working and tweak our model before pursuing its adoption as a country-wide education program. What we're doing is making a big difference, and years from now when this is quantifiable, it will be exciting to see how opportunities unfold to apply our model more widely across Ghana and other parts of the world.

CHAPTER FIVE

Luvudo

Winding through dense forests and banana groves down a deeply rutted, uneven trail, Luvudo is a jarring 25-minute drive from the closest paved road. It's a remote village in the Volta Region of Ghana and a beautiful setting despite its isolation. It is an agrarian village focused on providing food for its families, growing cocoa, coffee, cassava, and maize. Farm plots are often many miles away, requiring villagers to walk long distances in addition to doing backbreaking work all day. A nearby river provides a source of water. A unique feature of Luvudo is that the village is divided between a Muslim and a Christian section. But like Hehekpoe, they have the same desire to be known and to have a future filled with opportunity.

When we first encountered Luvudo, their only school, consisting of two three-room buildings for their K-6 students, was in disrepair, the roof and sides caved in on one of them. Children who made it past the sixth grade to junior high school faced treacherous conditions because children had to walk about four miles each way to the nearest school. During the rainy season, these kids had to cross a river and face a treacherous runoff from the surrounding mountains which would ultimately claim some of their lives.

When longtime Adanu volunteer, Betsy Benoit, first traveled to Luvudo in 2013, she was part of the first group of volunteers that had ever visited the village. Adanu was building a urinal as part of our assessment phase to determine whether the community was ready to build a school and a library. Luvudo appeared to have a lot of potential at that time and we were hopeful. Community members embraced our model by demonstrating a strong community work ethic and enthusiastic cooperation. This led to phase two: another group of volunteers and a new school.

Once the school was built, enrollment increased. Even when children

> **As we drove toward Luvudo, we were met by the entire community, singing and dancing as they led us the last 100 yards into the village. While we were there, they taught us their dances and songs. But there was so much more to learn from the people of Luvudo. They showed us joy, hope, and an abundance of determination. They knew education was the key to improving their children's future.**
>
> —BETSY BENOIT

are sick, they want to go to school. It's where they experience a lot of joy, and they don't want to miss even one day.

Jump ahead two years to an amazing amount of change. Adanu's collaboration with the community and the people's hard work resulted in the building of a school, as well a library that was filled with beautiful books through donations from many sources.

Adanu's work had served as a catalyst for change in the entire community. They'd set in motion clearing a plot of heavily forested land next to the old school and had planted cocoa trees and other saleable, edible crops for the benefit of the community as a whole. They'd constructed a new set of stairs to make access to the old school easier, and construction of a toilet block had begun. A bridge was underway to help children get to the junior high school safely during stormy weather. Luvudo had initiated all this work on its own, using what they learned from us. Recently they have started raising money and donations of supplies to build their own high school.

Increased enrollment has also garnered the attention of the municipality. Their school grew to 15 staff members and nine classes. Community leaders now see that a commitment to good teaching and learning is a life-giving endeavor, worthy of much celebration.

Adanu offers a blueprint for collaboration and fostering community, resulting in self-determination. We helped the community understand the benefits of pooling resources and working as a team to accomplish goals. They took that vision and made it their own, which is exactly what we hope occurs when we partner with the rural communities.

Positive Change for Students in Luvudo

Gaffy Tsitre is a 19-year-old student teacher in Luvudo, her hometown. She recounted to me what is what like growing up in Luvudo, without adequate buildings. Students were trying to learn while sitting outside in the wind and rain. Sickness was common, and healthcare costs were high. Often, schools were closed due to harsh weather.

From age three through junior high, Gaffy left her family in Luvudo to live with her aunt to go to school. Kids didn't have the opportunity to get a good education in Luvudo, and her parents wanted something better for her, so they sent her away. This was a common experience at that time for families that had access to help or money.

Gaffy returned to the Volta region to go to high school and has stayed in the community as she continues her education to become a teacher.

Initially, Gaffy didn't want to come back to Luvudo. But now, when she gets her teaching credential she plans to stay because she loves her home and the situation in the school. She has a special interest in teaching history so students know the stories of the past, such as the truth about the slave trade, an important part of Ghanaian history.

Students in Luvudo agreed education in the community has improved

I love teaching. The kids sing and smile. They put me in a good mood! It's good for you to share what you've learned, be lovely to them, and help them understand how to learn. I teach them that it doesn't matter what their condition is right now, and that through education, opportunity is created. The attitude of success comes from inside you but a good teacher can make the difference.

When children are happy and there's more to education in the classroom than just academics and learning, like dancing and drumming, it makes them want to come to school, even if their mom says no. Because of Adanu's help, kids are advocating for education on their own. —GAFFY TSITRE

❝ Our parents now support us in going to school. We're happy to be in school. Before Adanu, we had no help. The library has been a support to learning. Many students even go to secondary school in other places but use the library to study when they get home. After Adanu helped build the library, it galvanized people. Now families are supportive of kids learning. The library is central to the community. **❞**

—SIKIFU, SOPHIA, MIRANDA

since Adanu came to their community. Sophia Afeavonawo (age 13), Sikifu Bgondi (age 16), and Miranda Kotuuke (age 15) said before Adanu, there were no structures for classrooms and no library or books to read. They said education is important to students so they can become useful in the future.

Sikifu said he'd like to be a doctor to care for sick people. He said it was important he learn English for this profession. Sophia wants to be a teacher because she likes reading and working with kids. Miranda also said she'd like to be a teacher because she wants to teach children to read storybooks. She said she feels happy reading stories to them and wants to improve her own vocabulary. All students agree Adanu has vastly improved the educational conditions in Luvudo.

Students spoke highly of Luvudo's Adult Literacy Program. They want their parents to learn English so they can practice it at home. English is a universal language and speaking and writing it empowers you in the world. Sikifu said if his mother could learn English, she would be more involved in what he is learning. He said her being illiterate has made her feel inferior to him. But now that she is learning English, she has more confidence.

The Adult Literacy Program

Headmaster Samuel Edem Atitse, who volunteers with the Adult Literacy Program, echoes his students' point-of-view. Twenty-eight women are learning English three times per week on the days they don't go to the market. Their initial goal was to be able to speak both with their kids and Adanu volunteers. But they know that learning English will be empowering in many ways.

The Adult Literacy Program was initiated by one of the mothers who came to me and asked that I teach her English. The twenty-eight women in this program are so invested in it, they have even created pink uniforms that resemble their kids' school uniforms and they wear them every time they go to their classes.

Samuel shared that when he first arrived in Luvudo (2000), there was

> It was encouraging for Adanu to arrive and see the community embrace the collaborative approach Adanu teaches. Our community rallied together and demonstrated our commitment. Everything started to move forward from there.
>
> —SAMUEL EDEM ATITSE

only one other teacher at the school. The government needed people to teach in Luvudo but the lack of classrooms made it a discouraging placement for a teacher. He was teaching combined grades; it was a desperate situation. Community members saw no financial way to improve the situation; they felt it was the government's job to build a new school and the government had said no.

A Library for Coming Together

Early in 2014, community members asked Adanu to build a library since the impact from building a school had been so positive.

The entire community participated in the project and the library was built. Volunteers helped with both the school and library projects. Our partners at Alma College and Literacy Beyond Borders also helped, and friends donated over 5,000 books.

The day the volunteers arrived, loaded down with boxes of books, is a day I'll never forget. We placed all the boxes in the middle of a gathering attended by the entire community. As the books were unpacked and we began reading them to the children, excitement grew. Volunteers were surrounded by children listening and looking to see what was on the pages. Parents leaned over their children to get a look. Groups of the older men,

> The library was a dream come true. Our community embraced all the volunteers with open arms because we realize that others in the world know we exist. We feel important. Because of that, we want to give our love in return. It is all we have to give. What could be more important than that? Volunteers feel our love and take it back with them. Their lives are enriched by it.

—SAMUEL EDEM ATITSE

chiefs and elders started picking up books and were pouring through the pages, smiling and discussing what they were discovering from the pictures on the pages. As it grew dark, we finally had to force ourselves to leave as none of the villagers wanted the day to end. The library has become the cornerstone for the entire community.

Community Self-Reliance

One day a child fell down a steep incline on the hill on his way to the urinal in Luvudo. On its own, the community decided to build a stairway so students would be safer. Villagers' friends donated time to help. In one weekend, the project was completed. This project, while small, was organized by Samuel and the teachers, and demostrates how the community has learned self-reliance and leadership from Adanu. Its amazing how far they have come since the days of waiting for the government to build a new school.

Education is Sustainable

Chief Franklin K. Akangla agrees with Samuel and reiterates the positive changes since Adanu came to Luvudo. Prior to Adanu, there were no structures for education, so many children had to leave their families and the community to go away to school. Once Adanu helped build the school and library in Luvudo, students came back.

He agrees with what others have said about Adanu building strength within their community. After Adanu, he said the mortar of the community was created as they built the buildings together. They were very involved in working together. Before Adanu, bringing the community together for a common purpose was not effective.

Education is seen differently in Luvudo, too. Tutors and student-teachers volunteer their time at the library and the kids learn from them, sometimes at the encouragement of their parents because education is valued and given high regard.

Chief Akangla also pointed out that Adanu has helped build a long-range vision to better their local economy. In the past, the community's primary income has come from farming. But, as farming becomes more expensive, it will be less viable. Education leads to new and better opportunities.

Education Builds Community

Catherine Akangla, Luvudo leader of women and the village Chief's wife, said Luvudo first discovered Adanu from children outside of their community who put Luvudo's leaders in touch with them. Before Adanu, there was low participation in community improvement projects and the life of the people was difficult. After Adanu came and built the library, it revived life for everyone. Students started excelling academically and now they can speak and read English. She sees education as important because it gives students the kinds of skills they can use to come back to the village someday and care for children and the elders.

Catherine noted that it's important people from the west come help her

> I've seen in life that we are not all equal. Some people just have a natural ability to lead with vision and make their dreams come true. In communities like Luvudo we needed someone to help us see how our dreams can be turned into reality. Taking this kind of initiative on their own seemed impossible. But, when people came from the outside with a vision, and a way to make it happen and help, the people willingly followed them. It was invaluable. And now we know how to make things happen on our own. This is the ultimate gift Adanu brought to Luvudo.

—SAMUEL EDEM ATITSE

" Adanu shows kindness, compassion and the way they are feeling from the heart. They want to help us. When the volunteers come, our community cherishes it a lot. We give them gifts of oranges, bananas and a lot of ourselves. "

—CHIEF FRANKLIN K. AKANGLA

community because Luvudo lacks the financial capacity. It is also important for volunteers to interact with the children to receive love, and to witness how their effort and money is being used to make Luvudo stronger. When volunteers and Adanu come to Luvudo, they become brothers and sisters. We offer them our love.

" I appreciate the Adult Literacy Program because it's where I learned to write my ABCs and where I learned about manners, like saying please, thank you, I'm sorry, and good morning. When my kids come home from school, we are able to learn together. I've started speaking with small confidence. I smile now because I'm literate, which is important for everybody, not just the children. Others my age say they are too old to do it. But I know they can learn too. All of us are very grateful to Adanu. Always remember we love you. "

— CATHERINE AKANGLA

CHAPTER SIX

Kpedze-Todze

The smallest of the four communities that make up Kpedze-Todze is isolated, pristine, and far from any schools. Nestled in the mountains with a population of 552 people, Todze is largely a subsistence farming community, growing vegetables for their own use and small crops of plantain, banana, cassava, maize and cocoa for market sale. People here also raise goats, sheep and poultry, or work as carpenters, hairdressers, seamstresses and masons.

In order to provide much-needed local schooling for their children, the community initiated a building school project in 2002, but while the community was enthusiastic about the project, they ran out of funding.

Their village leader, Chief Okuma V, at the recommendation of one of his community members, planned to contact an organization in the Netherlands for funding. He wrote the letter, addressed it, and traveled the long distance to Ho to send the letter. That's when I met him while I was working at the cyber café. My youthful bravado and his willingness to take a risk on a young kid resulted in Adanu's second summer work camp with 30 volunteers. Together with numerous enthusiastic community members, we completed the long-stalled project in only one month.

We were impressed by the people's responsiveness to rallying around their chief and elders, and their willingness to mobilize for any type of activity, including hard labor.

This began an enduring 15-year relationship between Adanu and Kpedze-Todze which continues to this day. Our partnership is one of sharing, appreciation of each other and deep friendship. We have accomplished many other projects there, such as a canteen computer lab, urinals, a kindergarten block, and an improved sanitation facility.

We also introduced Chief Okuma V to Sylvia Morrison, who funded stocking of books at a library for the basic school and the construction of a bio-fill toilet facility for the school and community's use.

Additionally, we teamed the Kpedze-Todze community with Ryerson University in Canada. The University helped build a uniquely designed kindergarten, only the second of its kind in Africa. Adanu continues our investment with the school by providing donations of supplies like soccer balls and sports kits.

This relationship has so deepened that the community has recognized me with the distinction of being their Development Chief, renaming me Togbe Yingor, meaning "forever moving forward". Sylvia has also received equal distinction as Development Queen, honored under the name of Mama Agbalenyo-I due to her keen interest in encouraging the children of Todze to read.

Working alongside community members and the chief, we brought significant improvement to Kpedze-Todze. Their school is performing better now and the awareness of the importance of education is tremendous. Every year community members are excited to welcome new volunteers. As a matter of fact, collaboration with Adanu so excites members of the community that they are inspired to share what we do with neighboring communities and get those people connected too.

The Adanu and Kpedze-Todze's partnership has much evidence of its success on the ground. The library, computer lab, and other new facilities at the school have led to increased enrollment in Kpedze-Todze basic school, and improved quality of life in the village.

Women's Leadership

Margaret Akpabli, a woman leader at Kpedze-Todze says Adanu's partnership with their community has led to a significant boost in people working together. Women are vibrantly involved in building projects, fetching water, and mixing and carrying concrete alongside the men. Volunteers also ignite their community and inspire friendship, hospitality, and love.

Women's education is encouraged so girls can grow up to lead and be more useful, productive members of society, to their families, parents, and themselves. They're provided with equal opportunity to learn.

In 1921, the first vice principal of Achimota College in Accra, Dr. James Emman Kwegyir Aggrey, said, "If you educate a man, you educate an individual. But if you educate a woman, you educate a nation." Kpedze-Todze is turning this ideology into reality.

The Headmaster's Perspective

When I spoke with Amaoku John Yaw, Headmaster of Kpedze-Todze Basic school in Kpedze-Todze, he said Adanu has helped their community identify development projects that need to be done there. One project that has been identified is the need to build accommodations for staff. He emphasized the importance of having the headmaster and teachers living in the community where they teach.

He feels Adanu's priority of building urinals first to keep the environment clean and to involve the community in working together is essential. He values having a school that provides a comfortable place for learning and a playground for kids to socialize with each other. Additionally, he noted that the library Adanu helped build at Kpedze-Todze has given the children broad access to learning about educational disciplines as well as the world's places and cultures.

Educationally, since Adanu started working with Kpedze-Todze, the student's performance has excelled, recently shown by their success at an inter-school quiz competition. They rose to the third level, just shy of the finals. The school's quiz club keeps students learning and ready for many academic competitions and motivates kids to learn all the time.

The Kpedze-Todze community understands that education is key to the social, moral, and academic development of their children. To that end, past graduates become models for those still in school.

Rural vs. City Education

Tsitsia Delight, a student from the Assistant Girls Prefect, talked with me about the contrast between a private school she had previously attended and her experience going to the basic school in Kpedze-Todze. She said the basic school has trained teachers who know how to teach and deliver classroom instruction. Bogoso, on the other hand, was taught by former high school students with no teacher training.

Since it was a mining town, Bogoso was booming, bustling and extravagant. But it lacked the serenity and the deep sense of community of Kpedze-Todze. When she first came to Kpedze-Todze there was no library and the school buildings were substandard. Now the structure of the school has changed considerably, with new dedicated, committed teachers and a new headmaster. School performance has measurably improved, and parents are now enthusiastically enrolling their children.

These improvements are particularly important because Ghana has standardized national testing to measure students' knowledge and aptitude required for further education. Those who do well on the tests can move on, those who don't, can't. Also, when city kids' scores skew higher, their schools are far more likely to get government funding, compounding the problem since these schools will be able to offer their students even better buildings, more skilled teachers, and increased access to computers and up-to-date learning materials.

For this reason, Tsitsia believes rural children are at a considerable disadvantage over city kids in national tests. Because rural schools lack buildings, teachers, and materials they provide inferior preparation for the tests, score poorly, and, as a result, continue to be left out of additional resource allocations. Because of this, parents are forced to either send their kids to live with relatives in the cities or forgo their kids moving on to higher education. For some families who don't have relatives in a city, sending their kids away is simply not an option.

Tsitsia aspires one day to be a doctor. She wants people who read this book to know that Adanu engages kids in reading, as well as math, science and English. She said it is important for westerners to come here because they engage kids in reading and their interaction boosts students' confidence.

A Mother's Perspective

One mother I spoke to remembers what it was like in Kpedze-Todze before Adanu came here. Vinolia Dartney Adzanku said the community, despite being resolute and united, was economically challenged. Earning a living was difficult, depending mainly on sustenance farming.

Since Adanu arrived, there have been a lot of positive changes. Their school has new buildings, a computer lab, toilet facility for the school kids, a sanitation facility for the community's use, canteen for the kids and a library. The addition of a computer lab with access to the Internet brings the world that much closer for kids because it's just a click away.

Vinolia says volunteers are openly welcomed and loved because they bring inspiration and ideas for financially profitable development projects with them. She appreciates how easily they assimilate into the community.

Growing Up in Kpedze-Todze and Persevering

Kpedze-Todze student Peter Kwasi Adzido's story has similarities to my own. A 25-year-old Ghanaian who grew up in Kpedze, his motto describes the struggle he went through to obtain his education, "I may run through the nooks and crannies of this world with much sorrow, pain and agony, but my determination to become a hero will never end until someday I receive my crown."

Born to a roadside water and biscuit seller and a teacher, Peter's upbringing was under-privileged. When he wasn't in school, he helped his mother sell water, biscuits, and organic fertilizer on market days. When his mother went through a third caesarean and could not work anymore, his life became even more difficult. Like me, Peter realized early on the only way he could be successful was to be focused, determined, stay out of trouble, and remember his strong faith and values.

Peter's education began in an open-air classroom in Kpedze-Todze. He suffered the stigma of not attending a well-resourced preparatory school. In fact, life was so hard that he decided to drop out of school temporarily to do whatever he could to make money since that would at least give him food and relieve him of his educational struggles. His father's single income was supporting a sick mother, newborn baby, senior brother and his step-mom. There was scarce left over for his textbooks and school fees. But his dad knew the value of education and would trade him extra food for reciting his multiplication tables.

To keep body and soul alive, Peter became an errand boy for people in the neighborhood, fetching water, buying food for others, or working on their farms. He persevered. When Adanu came to his community and refurnished the dilapidated school, provided computers, stocked their library with books, and provided sports equipment, Peter's school experience at Kpedze-Todze changed markedly. Already a good student, in this new environment, he excelled. After several months of working without a dime, he resorted to selling top-up cards (pre-paid phone cards). Then he was accepted as a student to the Evangelical Presbyterian University College in Ho but could not afford to pay the one-hundred Ghana Cedis for his hostel room, about twenty-two dollars per term. Though he ultimately did make it through a four-year Business Administration program, finances were always a big challenge.

In addition to the financial struggle, he was often ostracized by classmates because of his clothing and his roommate said his rice was "too local and not fit for consumption." I can imagine how hurtful that must have been to him, particularly since his parents never had enough to eat and were severely ridiculed by lenders just to provide him with enough money for textbooks. He was even evicted from a lecture hall due to his inability to buy a communications skills handout and nearly ejected from the examination hall because he could not finish paying a net balance of 300 Ghana Cedis (about 70 US Dollars).

Peter says Adanu inspired him to study hard so he could one day prove that he could be successful no matter where he came from or who his parents were. We encouraged him to never accept mediocrity, and to know that every person is the architect of his/her own future.

Despite the challenges he went through, Peter has experienced great success. When he graduated with First Class Honors in Human Resource Development and Management in 2013/14, he also received the university's Best Student Award. He credits Adanu with helping him achieve the strong foundation to make this possible.

Today, Kpedze-Todze has a kindergarten, primary school and junior high school. The junior high school provides children with a computer lab, library, ample classroom space and good teachers. In fact, the school in Todze has such a good reputation for education, it not only educates local children, but also students from neighboring towns.

Currently, after the basic examinations, senior high school students attend school in neighboring towns to further their educations. As a community, most people acquire a basic education. And the fact there are no households in the Kpedze-Todze community that don't have at least one graduate from a university, college, or polytechnic is a testament to the value this community places on education.

The results of Adanu's partnership with Kpedze-Todze are far-reaching and can be seen in the influence this community now has in Ghanaian society. In addition to people like Peter, the Commander of the Ghana Navy and the Chief Director of the Ghana Meteorological Department also come from Kpedze-Todze, as well as other noted financial and educational leaders.

When volunteers are interested in traveling from outside Ghana to help, this lifts the people's view of their own value and gives them confidence. Exposure to the outside world has changed the mindset of people living in Kpedze-Todze. Inter-relationships, sharing of ideas and working on development with volunteers from all walks of life has affected the community positively and encouraged them to extend their talents beyond their community throughout Ghana.

PART III

More Partnerships

"by God's grace, all will be well"
Adinkra symbol of hope, providence, and faith

CHAPTER SEVEN

University Engagement and Community Collaboration

In 2014 the New York University (NYU) Stern Business School offered an international volunteer seminar (called SIV) when Professor Rachel Kowal brought a group of students to Ghana. It was after this initial trip that her vision for collaboration with Adanu and the community of Woadtze-Tsatoe came together. She and her colleague Professor Hans Taparia established a five-year (2015-2020) partnership with Adanu to improve education, potable water, healthcare, and microbusiness in Woadze-Tsatoe.

The goals of the immersive experience are to teach social entrepreneurship research to the students as a tool for evaluating what they observed on the ground in Ghana, provide volunteer support to an Adanu project, and simply engage with the community of Woadze-Tsatoe.

Woadze-Tsatoe, a fishing community with a population of 500 people, may seem like an unlikely study destination for a group of students from a university business school. Nestled along Lake Volta, there are no concrete structures, paved roads, or even a health clinic. But this is precisely why NYU believed the environment was appropriate for studying and introducing social entrepreneurship.

The NYU experience is academic and gives volunteers a cultural experience, but it also gives those who participate a golden opportunity to watch the Adanu model unfold and succeed.

To qualify for a partnership with Adanu and NYU, the village chief and elderly council had to express a desire to work together over the entire project cycle, provide managerial oversight of the projects, and commit human resources of the village for their construction. Though community led, they also needed to understand that Adanu reserves the right to supervise and direct all critical stages of the project and check with working committee leaders to keep track of their progress and material needs. The Woadze-Tsatoe chief and elder council were eager to make this commitment.

In 2015, the first step of this partnership was to use Adanu's model on a small project to assess the community's commitment. Villagers and students molded bricks, carried water, and built a urinal, which became the first concrete structure in the village. The success of this first project set the stage for the five-year partnership. We set in motion plans to build a school in the village.

At the same time, the NYU students conducted research on the need for and availability of healthcare, education, sanitization, and clean water for the village. They would take their findings back to their classroom in New York with a plan to return in 2016 with options to address the community's needs, including volunteering with an Adanu project to construct a school and helping the community implement business ventures.

Students collected data on possible social enterprises, breaking up into teams that engaged in observation, interviewing, and business model exercises to determine possible micro-enterprises for Woadze-Tsatoe, as well as a few surrounding villages.

Teams explored numerous possibilities, ranging from aquaculture on nearby Lake Volta to solar energy generation. The team's findings also identified a need for clean water. Women, they discovered, had the time and desire to work. Plus, students learned from both observation and from talking with the community that people valued education but the village lacked a permanent school structure and resources to provide it.

In the end, the collaboration between students and the community resulted in the decision to build a three-unit classroom block with offices, a batik manufacturing center, and a water system with a holding tank and multiple faucets to provide the community with potable water.

NYU also brought low-cost computers to set up in the school, for both educational and business uses. This project was facilitated through the Adanu model of community involvement, with the students helping both with manual labor as well as developing lessons and providing resources for the school's four dedicated teachers to use.

Student Karan Magu shared about his experience:

Two days into my trip to rural Ghana when I arrived in Woadze-Tsatoe village, I realized I was many hours away from urban life as I knew it. Armed with gallons of bug spray, I was ready for the blistering heat but not the torrents of rain pouring through the village; it was nothing like New York City.

I spent two weeks in Woadze-Tsatoe developing projects with Adanu as part of my NYU class. As the bus bumped up into the village, the words of my friend Chris, an administrator at NYU Acrra, rang in my ears, "Patience will be your middle name." I'd chosen a career path that involves providing digital technology to disconnected places, but I wasn't sure I'd survive this trip. Shortly into it, however, I changed my mind.

Karan's volunteerism at Woadze-Tsatoe confirmed his theory that given the right environment and basic infrastructure, it is possible for anyone to learn how to interact with technology, even without prior experience. Through support and encouragement from his professors and contributions from classmates, their group donated three laptops to the village school. In a community where fishing and farming had forever been the only future available to the children, the possibility of working at an IT company, whether as an administrator, an engineer, or a programmer was opened.

In 2016, when students arrived the community had already begun preparing for the students' arrival.

Children hovered around as I introduced them to a laptop computer and its wonders. As they touched the keys and learned about software, they were excited and rapt with attention. Many of the kids had never seen a computer, much less touched one. By the end of the first day, most of them could write word documents on my computer.

—KARAN MAGU, Student, New York University (NYU) Stern School of Business in an article for *The Gould Standard*

Water Company

The main project for the incoming NYU student volunteers was to help the community set up a water company with a goal of making it self-sufficient and sustainable. Demonstrating the Adanu model at work, villagers had worked with the help of Clean Water for Everyone and put a water pump in place and installed a water tank and faucets.

The goal was to build a mechanized pump and tank to create a business that could sell clean water to nearby villages. SIV students discovered that development institutions and governments tended to construct water pumps in villages worldwide that eventually broke down. Without adequate funds to repair them, the water pumps stood dormant and unused. Woadze-Tsatoe's elder council suggested the idea of setting a water pump up as a business, charging people a nominal amount for drinking water to ensure a funding source for future maintenance.

While the SIV group was a bit anxious to see how the leadership would come together, they quickly discovered their fears were unfounded. They discovered that in a village with virtually no connectivity and nothing else for people to focus on, a lot could be accomplished in six days. Because the community was already engaged in and given agency to take control of these enterprises, the governance and leadership discussions went quickly and smoothly. In the end, the board decided to charge competitive prices for the water pumping service they were providing; money was already starting to come to the village.

A moment of truth came on the second day when the students and Professors Kowal and Taparia engaged the elder council in a discussion on governance and leadership. Creating the right templates for how these businesses would be run and by whom would be critical to the

> We needed to delicately engage the village in a dialogue about leadership and governance, and we needed to test numerous business assumptions. We also needed to ensure that each operation had started before we left.
>
> —PROFESSORS RACHEL KOWAL AND HANS TAPARIA

long-term success and sustainability of the enterprises. It was a high-level discussion, except they were sitting under a tree with the sound of roosters crowing and babies crying in the distance, the village council on one side, and their class of 30 participants on the other.

The students had begun drafting principles and processes that would help inspire the village to create their own leadership structure, including boldly suggesting they appoint women to roles of leadership, both at the board and operating levels. The conversations were productive and within a day, the village Council had appointed boards for both the water company and a batik center with women in the majority holding prominent leadership roles.

The NYU professors, students, and village leaders were pleased with the quick success.

Batik Manufacturing Center

A batik training program began that very day involving 34 women. Within hours, bright colors and intricate designs were catching the gaze of everyone in the village. There are few words to describe the enthusiasm of the women, but the sight of a woman dying fabric while simultaneously breastfeeding perhaps best captured the moment. Community engagement was obvious, as was the benefit this would have on the village.

The community's vision for the batik business was to create batik fabric they would turn into goods designed by the New York-based design company Studio 189. Village women would then sell the goods back to Studio 189, where they would be finished and re-sold.

This business and collaboration was viewed as a culturally appropriate one since batik is an ancient Ghanaian tradition of colorful block printing and dyeing on cotton. Studio 189, spearheaded by NYU Stern alumnus Abrima Erwiah and actress Rosario Dawson, already worked with women's groups across Ghana to source traditional designs and manufacture high-end fashion products for global consumers. NYU students worked to develop a business plan for the new enterprise. Fabric and pareos made in Woadze-Tsatoe would be made into products at the Studio 189 production factory in Accra and sold online. Studio 189 also committed to playing a

" Working with NYU and Adanu has brought a lot of exciting change in the community. To have volunteers in the village builds very good relationships. They come into the houses, help the people cook, go to the river with us, and are a part of our lives. Our community is very happy about this because the volunteers bring happiness, gladness, and light with them. This is a present to the community. We hope they will continue coming. "

—BATIK ARTIST, WOADZE-TSATOE

role on the board of the new village enterprise.

The partnership between Adanu and NYU helped build the local batik manufacturing center in Woadze-Tsatoe. Today it has become a successful micro-business on its own, independent of Studio 189, named Amenuveve, which means "grace."

The batik center runs three days a week for six hours, giving the village consistent income. Amenuveve has also promised that a percentage of its profits will go to Woadze-Tsatoe's school and community projects.

One day when I visited the Woadze-Tsatoe batik center, I saw yards of white cloth stretched along long tables. With their hands wrapped around carved wooden stamps, the women batik artists pressed swirling images of hot wax into the lengths of it, then dipped the sheets into plastic buckets of deep, colorful plant dye. With every new added color, the women's work became more challenging. After dying was complete, the cloth was boiled to remove the wax. Batik images are geometric forms designed for their beauty, or can be images symbolic of historical events, customs, beliefs or special occasions. Their colors can sometimes even carry meaning.

This collaboration shows the Adanu model working successfully, particularly when paired with social entrepreneurship that has the potential to become a sustainable source of income.

The Flow of Entrepreneurship

Professors Kowal and Taparia described the change in their perspective during one of their evening reflection sessions. The weight of what they were trying to do had settled in. Adanu's relationship with the NYU Stern School of Business had become more than a class. There was uncertainty, of course, but students were committed to do everything in their power to make the collaboration successful.

The shared perspective is that these businesses, when implemented well, could support the community and pay for advancements. Evidence is proving this to be accurate. By the end of the 2016 program, the governing structures for both businesses were in place and operating.

Yet it is not just the Woadze-Tsatoe villagers who have benefitted from this experience. The students have learned that the language of business is universal. They have been able to practice the concepts they learned in school in an environment where they can create real, sustainable change.

Holy Agbaadsi, Assistant Headmaster and teacher at Woadze-Tsatoe, said after Adanu and NYU helped Woadze-Tsatoe build a classroom and donated school materials, boxes of school supplies, and the computers, her students became eager to learn communication technology. They are now much better prepared for the world.

Adanu and the NYU Stern School of Business have worked together to empower Woadze-Tsatoe through both business and social projects. But the students who participated in the SIV are also empowered. They are invested in seeing that their ideas are brought to fruition. They are committed to helping make a significant and sustainable change through social

> By working deeply in a microcosm, we are better able to see the bigger picture. We all have epiphanies and realize that whatever we do, we must make life count. We can see that the exchange has been mutual. We can see that over two years of work, the community has been touched. An ecosystem has been established. There is an air of aspiration.
>
> —RACHEL KOWAL & HANS TAPARIA

“ Before Adanu and NYU came to Woadze-Tsatoe, the children had no interest in education. They didn't like coming to school. But now they do. They are interested and willing to be in school. The lives of the volunteers were also changed. They learned about life at Woadze-Tsatoe, about fishing, going to the river, cooking, how to speak our language, Ewe, and other cultural experiences. They expanded their minds. ”

—HOLY AGBADSI

entrepreneurship, and they now consider themselves part of a global community as they graduate and move on to whatever their career may bring.

The Power of Collaboration and Student Engagement

The result of this ongoing collaboration continues to demonstrate the power of entrepreneurship. With Adanu's help and guidance, the NYU team has offered a path toward economic advancement that will inspire and support a community beyond NYU or Adanu's involvement, much in the same way Adanu has been working with multiple communities around Ghana.

As a business student interested in development economics, SIV student Jordan Wolken recognized volunteering at Woadze-Tsatoe was a beneficial way to see an alternative, hands-on approach to development aid. He noted the work NYU Stern School of Business and Adanu do in Woadze-Tsatoe is empowering women in the village, creating sustainable businesses, enhancing clean water, and providing education resources with far less funding than other multilateral organizations.

Jordan was so inspired by his trip to Ghana that he is interning with Adanu in the U.S. to create more university partnerships like he experienced with the NYU SIV program. He hopes to take his intern experience at Adanu and apply it to work with a tutoring non-profit organization serving low-income students in New York City.

University students who participate in Adanu programs express their pleasant surprise with the welcoming, open, friendly spirit of the Ghanaian people. Treated as part of the community, they said their immersive experience helped them see more closely how a social enterprise worked and enriched their lives with new friendships and cultural understanding. Conclusively, they said their experience in Ghana gave them a clearer understanding of what it means to do well by doing good through volunteerism.

Along with making new friendships, they mentioned the frustration of trying to communicate with villagers who did not speak English. Smiles went a long way to foster communication when language was a barrier. Volunteers also said being present in Ghana was far more valuable in person than through email. The trip helped put their personal goals in perspective, and for that, they were grateful to Adanu and the communities where they served.

> I want to share my amazing experience with others who are unfamiliar with Adanu. More specifically, I'd like to tell others about how cultural immersion programs like Adanu's are more fulfilling than traditional tourism or even traditional volunteerism. Pitching the SIV Ghana program to my personal network and those at other universities will hopefully inspire others to work with Adanu.

—JORDAN WOLKEN

CHAPTER EIGHT

Working with Government for Sustainable Change

Ghana has a national policy of free and compulsory education for all K-12 students. There is ambiguity around what "free" actually means as virtually all schools charge some fees; however, all government agencies in Ghana say education is a top priority. Nonetheless, the reality is that funding is stretched tight and there is more need than the government can address on its own. This is felt no more acutely than in the Volta Region. The lack of education infrastructure is a big problem in the region, especially in the rural communities.

The government struggles to provide funds to build schools and provide teachers and teaching materials, and the rural communities are the ones that get left behind most often. Occasionally, funds are approved to build a school for a village. The government builds the school building through a local or regional contractor. If a community happens to get a job with the contractor, its people can work on the project. However, most often, the community is not allowed to take part in the work.

The reality is that most rural communities have endured decades of broken governmental promises regarding education, and school building projects. Adanu's vision is for people to work together to make projects happen, not to become stymied when the government can't meet their needs. Our approach offers communities a way to break this cycle and bring about effective teaching and learning in a safe, sound environment. Our approach aligns with the policy of our government. By providing school infrastructure to rural communities that the government is unable to support, we uphold their objectives. Each step of the way we work hard to collaborate with government officials. This opens awareness for the communities' other needs, and often inspires these officials to intervene and provide services such as clean water, healthcare, and roads.

By maintaining positive relations with local and federal government officials, Adanu is able to solicit their help in areas such as providing funding for additional teachers and learning materials. Government also provides personnel to supervise and monitor teaching and learning in schools built by Adanu. In some cases the government has provided crushed rock and other materials when the community was not able to provide them on their own.

Over the years, we have built solid bonds of friendship with Ghana's Agotime-Ziope District Mayor, Hon Adzaho, and Honorable Kwame Agbodza, Member of Parliament of Adakle District. Whenever we reach out to them, they are ready to help and support us to the extent they are able. They have always been committed to providing the necessary resources for projects. Likewise, they reach out to Adanu when faced with challenges in communities needing support within their area.

This mutually supportive collaboration helps Adanu become aware of other communities that are in need and strengthens our relationships with existing communities. Also, due to continuous engagement, it promotes easy understanding of our process, gives our work national recognition, and helps spread the news about our model with other politicians. Government officials' support and promotion of our work is beginning to facilitate wider acceptance of what we do and has been a source of encouragement to other communities and organizations to adopt the Adanu model.

Our Partnership with the Honorable Kwame Agbodza

Member of Parliament of Adakle District, which is part of the Volta Region and where Hehekpoe is located, Kwame Agbodza works alongside Adanu to address the challenges of education in his district. Passionate about Adanu's approach to development, he says our work is invaluable in Ghana because in addition to helping the government fill gaps in financial resources, we engage communities. He loves how we foster collaboration in our work and he sees the difference when community members are motivated to participate in the work, embrace and maintain the school infrastructure, and even initiate additional follow-up projects on their own.

Educated in London and a successful architect, Kwame understands the importance of proper facilities and infrastructure. Despite not having the ability to help financially, he supports us where he can. He wants to be a part of something that's successful, so he's publicly using his platform to endorse working with Adanu. He shares our belief that rural Ghanaian communities can only emerge from their challenges and embrace a better future through education and self-determination. He starts many conversations with constituents by letting people know about Adanu. We share a common commitment and work well together.

When we met Kwame in 2013, he had already determined education was going to be his platform while in office, and that his biggest challenge would be to provide good education to the children in his region. He wanted to "turn around the fortunes of the people in our community" and bring them better opportunities. He'd heard about the work Adanu was doing and was interested in exploring the idea of working with us.

Early on in his political career, he'd visited one school in the district and noticed the teachers didn't have any chalk. He then went to the District Office of Education and found a large pile of chalk. This helped him see the importance of self-determination and empowerment in a simple way. While it is the government's responsibility to provide schools with learning materials, including basics like chalk, the teachers weren't asking for what they needed. This is an example of what we are tyring to do at Adanu, and why I believe lasting change must come from building confidence, self-respect and dignity one village at a time. You might think chalk is a small thing, but when Kwame told me this story I knew what Adanu is doing was part of the answer, and I could clearly see how our model would help build confidence in teachers so they would feel comfortable about asking for supplies. If a village can build a school, in spite of the government's broken promises, a teacher can have the confidence to ask for chalk when she needs it.

In his first project with us, Kwame was impressed that people used local resources, sand, water and crushed rocks to shape blocks for their building. However, since this was a new way for him to work with a community and he didn't understand the pace and complexity of the Adanu Model, things didn't go as smoothly as he'd hoped. However, subsequent projects have been much better organized because he educates rural communities first about Adanu's approach and our expectations of them before we go there.

We recently went with him to three communities he wanted to serve. One of these was Adaklu Dawanu. Like so many of the rural villages we'd seen, the need in Dawanu was substantial. Kids were attending classes under trees, weren't properly dressed for school, and many were hungry. School materials were outdated and sometimes there weren't even teachers to teach the classes. The roads leading into Dawamu were simply rutted cattle tracks. Fresh palm branches held leaning huts together, obviously tossed together hastily before his visit, indicating no actual school existed. When Kwame visited the villages, parents sent their children out to represent them, rushing quickly back inside their homes.

In Adaklu Avelebe, three volunteer teachers, (two men and one woman) were eager to hear how Kwame and Adanu planned to build a school in their village. But because their existing school wasn't a state-recognized school and no government teachers taught there, Kwame was not allowed to use government money for the project. However, his commitment to the success of the village was so deep, he dug into his own pocket to give the teachers stipends for two months so they could continue to teach in the community while Adanu worked with the village to build a new school.

At the end of the project, a beautiful kindergarten school graced the village. Kwame continued partnering with Adanu to build a first-through-third grade classroom. Within four months, this had been accomplished.

Then we were told the community needed three more classrooms, for fourth, fifth and sixth grades. The new structures had caught the attention of parents in the community who now saw the value of sending their children to school. Kwami said the success was bittersweet, though. On the one hand, the facilities for education had improved. On the other, enrollment had doubled, leaving classrooms crowded with a need for more resource materials.

But increased enrollment and solid infrastructure had given legitimacy to the school, so the government became willing to send paid teachers. Kwame said he thought teachers who had been sent to Adaklu Avelebe might have felt resentment at being uprooted from urban areas to work in a remote, rural environment with poor conditions, no housing, and a drive every day down a broken, rutted, poor excuse for a road. He was surprised to discover they weren't angry at all. The teachers' main concern was a good education for the children. All they wanted to hear was that we were committed to helping them solve problems. So grading the road became Kwame's next endeavor, making transportation a bit easier. Now he is encouraging Adaklu Avelebe to build local accommodations for the teachers so they can live within the community.

Kwame notices a big change in the community. He sees joy in the people's faces. They believe they are blessed. People learned skills from working on the project they can sell to others in the future. They are completely committed to believing the school works for them. Unlike experiences with other NGOs that come and build a building and leave, communities sense Adanu's loyalty and commitment to their village, and it fills them with hope.

For the first time, schools have now been built in the Adaklu District. Kwame is looking forward to measuring further success of Adanu's work through test measurements, which is the way Parliament uses to determine if what we've done has made a difference. I have no doubt he will be happy with the scores. We have already improved teaching materials, teacher's training and infrastructure, and have seen much improvement. It's clear when we build the schools and engage the teachers, the schools grow and students excel.

In the future, Kwame said he'd like to see government funds allocated to rural areas for public transit so people will have easier access to the marketplace to sell their produce. He'd also like to see improvements to water supplies as a strategy for keeping people healthy. Money generated by increased access to the market and fresh water could then be used to further education. He'd also like to see more villages utilizing new technologies.

> Don't you think this would be a better world if all of us gave what we receive back to another generation?
>
> —HONORABLE KWAME AGBODZA

CHAPTER NINE

Looking to the Future

Adanu has been the silver lining in my life. I have always wanted to create something positive from the strife I endured growing up. My education made all the difference for me, and a passion for helping other children was born. I believed collaboration, hard work, and personal and community responsibility could be used to change the world for my people, one village at a time.

The beauty of it all is that I am now doing just what I dreamed of, through Adanu. The team and I are proud of Adanu and the work we do empowering rural, disadvantaged communities in Ghana through grassroots solutions.

I remember the immense happiness I felt after completing our first school building and the thrill of bringing those first international volunteers over to participate. Our friends did not know why we were doing what we were doing but their curiosity made them want to be around us and our newly-found "yevu" friends, the Ewe word for white people. It has all been so much fun, in spite of how hard it is and how much struggle we have endured. And to this day, every successful project still feels like a huge accomplishment. Adanu has served over 50 communities throughout the Volta region of Ghana. We have also hosted over 1,000 international volunteers.

In many ways it still feels like we are just getting started. My greatest hope is that the Adanu Model will be adopted by others in Ghana so that the rural impoverished communities who are still struggling will experience the benefits of the Adanu Model and all that proper education has to offer their children, and their communities as a whole.

I have become convinced we can't do it alone. We need local and central government to get on board more fully. And we need other NGOs to see how powerful our model is and begin promoting and delivering "helping that helps", even if that means adapting our model to fits their needs. And, as always, we need more donors and volunteers to help reduce the stack of hundreds of requests waiting for Adanu's "helping that helps."

As I put down my pen, I am still holding you with both hands, hoping this book has been as much a blessing to read as it was to write.

* * *

Adanu invites you to go to

https://www.adanu.org

to learn how you can participate in supporting our organization.
We could not do what we do without the support and
belief volunteers and sponsors have in our vision.
We offer our warmest invitation to you to join us.

AFTERWORD

----

*"Starting a non-profit requires hard
work, patience and a strong mission,
to which you must always be faithful."*

—Shelly Morse

A single shaft of warm light spills through the screened window beside my bed. Waking slowly on a bed with a wooden frame and one-inch pad, I look around the tiny square room. It's humid and hot and there's no air-conditioning. Outside, roosters crow loudly, announcing the day like persistent, tiny alarm clocks. In Hehekpoe, Ghana, days begin early. Children start school at 8:00 am.

A woman who has traveled with me from the United States is still asleep in the single bed adjacent to mine. It's her first time to Ghana and this village. Along with other volunteers and people from the community, she'll be helping build cement blocks for the foundation of a new water system for their primary school. I'm excited to share Ghana with her, a place with incredible people, where I am involved doing community development in a meaningful, sustainable, and respectful way.

Gentle stirrings come from the next room as Dina prepares a breakfast of Koko (fermented maize porridge) and plantain (cooked banana.) A woman with a beautiful smile and melodic voice, she talks softly with her husband Cephas, a strong, physically-fit man with a shaved head. Their words are indiscernible.

Dina's five-year-old twin girls, Rosemary and Rosemand, giggle outside my door. They're expectantly waiting for our morning ritual to get ready for the day. Due to our western modesty and the fact the toilet and shower are combined, we've been sitting on stools to bathe outside under the window, fully clothed. Rosemary, Rosemand, and their sisters, Emmaunella, ten years old, and Edem, twelve years old, carry large buckets of water to dump on us and laugh hysterically at our odd showering routine.

I remember when I first met the girls, wide-eyed and smiling, their hair shaved short. They had hesitantly peeked out at me from inside the house, trying to speak English. Helen, their grandma, a slim, sun-worn woman, had been even shyer because she spoke no English. Always welcoming, however, their generosity and warmth of spirit was characteristic of the Ghanaian people. Within minutes their simple, 200-foot rectangular house felt like home.

Years ago, my husband Clint, our daughter, Julia, and I traveled to Ghana as volunteers where we met Richard and Robert and became acquainted with Adanu. We felt an instant connection with them after seeing the team's hearts and experiencing their model of community development. They were working with little to no funding, yet persisted in their vision.

At its core, Adanu's model for helping people create lasting change requires convincing those they serve to rise to the challenge of helping themselves. Even in America, this is not an easy task where chronic poverty, hunger, homelessness, and educational struggles abound. But in Ghana, where resources and infrastructure are bare, this task can seem insurmountable. Creating a permanent solution—*helping that helps*—is definitely hard work, but hope is a powerful weapon, one that Adanu uses effectively.

Success for Adanu hasn't been immediate. This book could have highlighted as many failures as successes:

- the heartache of working with a community that didn't follow through on its commitment to participate in a project

- the disappointment of having to tell a village that funding fell through after beginning a project

- the weather and other natural disasters that complicate the already hard work of building in a rural village without modern equipment.

Over the years I have wished we could fix the problems in Ghana with western innovation and ideas, frustrated by how hard a path Adanu had chosen. I have wished they could work more efficiently, wished more people would help, hoping these impoverished communities could be freed from their difficulty sooner. I have come to realize that Adanu has had it right all along. I am convinced lasting change must come from inside Ghana, from each village, and ultimately from inside the hearts and minds of everyone in the community, one by one.

Adanu is pursuing its mission in a worldwide culture where there are many voices promoting an easier, faster way. The politicians in Ghana promise, repeatedly, that they will provide the help needed, but they simply don't have the resources. Other

> **The most terrible poverty is loneliness and the feeling of being unloved.**
>
> — MOTHER TERESA

well-intentioned organizations promise to help, without requiring the personal commitment the Adanu model requires. Even many in the Christian church in Ghana promise help from God if only you pray hard enough or have enough faith. The villages Adanu serves hear these voices and become convinced they can't help themselves, that the best or only path is to wait for others to help them. Despite all of this, Adanu has remained faithful to its vision that self-reliance is the best path to dignity, hope and lasting change in Ghana.

The work Adanu does is not simply aid, a hand-out, or an invasion. It is Ghanaian-led development born out of friendship and relationship and I feel honored to play a smart part of the work. Our partnership forces me to examine who I am, in a good way. I'm inspired every day by the courage and grit I see in Richard and his team. These men are educated and extremely talented. They could do any work they choose but they selflessly help their people create opportunity. They inspire me to look at my own life and be courageous.

I trust God with all the different pieces of my life, the good and the bad, from the beginning to the end. Instinctively, I knew Adanu was going to be one of my life's essential pieces, and to this day, it is. I connect with the lifestyle and people in Ghana in a deep way. They're hard to shake. I can't forget what I've seen and those I've met. Their dreams inspire me and the hope they have for their children and themselves spurs me on. They're courageous people and what they face makes me ask myself, "What am I afraid of?" I want to walk alongside these hard-working people, offering them friendship, encouragement, and resources. Ghana has touched my soul.

We all have resources for change regardless of our circumstances. Adanu helps people in Ghana take personal responsibility to make changes in their lives and communities, and helps them believe that they are worthy of it. But if any of us are to embrace change, we must take that first step to be involved. The invitation to you to join Adanu as a volunteer on the ground in Ghana is the same invitation Adanu offers communities throughout the Volta Region: Choose to live differently even if you've never thought it was possible.

Volunteering with Adanu is a beautiful opportunity to work within a successful community development model, immersed in the Ghanaian culture with people who are authentic. The opportunity is a rare experience in today's world. It's an excellent place to begin examining your capacity for doing good and to become aware of how your participation can help others. But, if it's not right for you, I encourage you to discover what is.

This book is an invitation to serve. Maybe you won't volunteer with Adanu and experience Ghana. But perhaps by reading Adanu's story, a place will awaken in you that hasn't been open before and you will be inspired to give of yourself to others. This is my greatest hope.

—Shelly Morse

THE ADANU TEAM

Empowering Communities Together

Robert Tornu, Director of Community Coordination, received a college degree in Adult Education from the University of Ghana. Access to quality education, clean water, and opportunities that build a strong, positive foundation for women and children are among his top priorities.

Mypa Winfred Kofi Buckner, Director of Operations, holds a Higher National Diploma (HND) in Marketing from the Ho Polytechnic in the Volta Region, Ghana. Currently pursuing his degree in Human Resource Management, he has been president of a local wing of the LEO club, a youth segment of the Lions Club International, for two terms.

Emmanuel Awline, Transport Director, is so easy-going, people wonder if he's ever been annoyed. A responsible, dedicated driver, he spends much of his time at work. Since he drives for very long hours without getting tired, to "rest," he plays football during his leisure time. As a Christian, he abhors lies and laziness and often says, "Laziness is a crime punishable by poverty."

Akah Angelbert Elorm "DJ," Director of Construction, has a keen interest in politics, current affairs, technology, music and sports. He is inspired by Adanu's friendship, unity, and passion to help others in need, and loves to have fun while achieving high-quality results. He holds a BSC in Building Technology from the Kwame Nkrumah University of Science and Technology in Ghana.

Bright Kwasi Tay, Logistics Officer, joined Adanu to help bring opportunity to rural people in the Volta Region, Ghana. Finding joy in the happiness of others, Bright is passionate about football. Whenever he passes kids playing *gutter to gutter*, he takes time to watch and will recommend talented ones to the established soccer clubs. As a Christian, he also enjoys music and quiet time with God.

Betsy Benoit, Director, Friends of Adanu, holds a BA in Liberal Arts and Sciences from the University of Hawaii at Manoa. After her third trip with Adanu, she decided its mission fit her life dreams. She eagerly shares the organization's vision both locally and globally, collaborating with others to gain greater sustainable education and development in communities that have been overlooked in the past.

Please join us

www.adanu.org

ACKNOWLEDGMENTS

Thank you to:

God, for life

Amedzofe community and its risk-taking chief

Kpedze-Todze community

Adaklu Hehekpoe community

Patience Yinkah, my auntie, for providing Adanu's first office

All the communities Adanu has served in its 15-year history

Our many partners, especially Mosaic, District/Municipal Assemblies, members of Parliament of all the communities Adanu has served, Ghana Education Service, Volta Regional Coordinating Council, Ghana Library Board

All the volunteers who have served the Volta Region communities for 15 years, especially Jamie Piekarz, Lori Beckstead, Helga Liz Haberfellner, Paul Andrew, Jill Dempsey, Laura Baxter, Margit Boyesen, Joanne Provo, David and Maria Floud, Adam Williams, Rodrigo Cobo, Christopher Deha, Tom Gerber, Liz Hilton, David Levine, Christa E. Sanders, Myriam Chabani, Diego Cobo, and Signe Nellemann

New York University (NYU) Accra, NYU Stern School of Business students and Professors Rachel Kowal & Hans Taparia

Going, Going Ghana Canada Team

Links Across Borders

The Mosaic Company volunteers

GlobeAware

Global Hope Alliance

Bright Light Volunteers

Tremitiere Family

Trip of A Life Time

Adanu's Ghanaian Team: Robert Tornu, Bright Kwasi Tay, Akah An-gelbert "DJ" Elorm. Emmanuel Awline, Mypa Kofi Buckner, and Jerry Kotoka

Blessed memory of Divine "star-watcher" Agbowoada

Mario Valentino, Adanu's photographer, and Anku and Nelson Aga-mah of MAV Films GH

Friends of Adanu in the United States and Betsy Benoit

And, to those who helped make the book happen: Clint Morse, Shelly Morse, and Karen Lynn Maher

ABOUT THE AUTHORS

Richard Yinkah is the founder and executive Director of Adanu. He holds a college degree in Integrated Development Studies from Evangelical Presbyterian University College. He is currently studying for a master's degree in Governance and Sustainable Development at the University of Cape Coast.

His entrepreneurial spirit and tenacity have grown Adanu from a small organization headquartered in his aunt's store room to a thriving organization positively impacting communities across Ghana. His passion and mission is to give children in his country opportunities he fought so hard for during the early years of his life. He believes collaboration, hard work and education can change the world, one village at a time. This is his first book.

Shelly Morse is a primary benefactor of Adanu. She is mother of four, grandmother of five and is deeply loyal to her family. She is a spiritual guide to those navigating life's challenges. In Ghana, they call her Mama Shelly.

Karen Lynn Maher owns LegacyONE Authors Publishing in Kirkland, Washington. She guides thought leaders to write nonfiction books that share their story and convey their expertise.